Private Equity
How the Business of Private Equity Funds Works

Daniel Burmester

Copyright © 2012 Daniel Burmester

All rights reserved.

ISBN: 1545499969
ISBN-13: 978-1545499962

"I have never let my schooling interfere with my education"

Mark Twain

Contents

1 Introduction 9
    Historic development of private equity 10
    Differences between private equity, venture capital, and hedge funds 12
    Private Equity - Greed for profit to the cost of employees? 15
    The private equity landscape 18
    The typical career path in private equity 23
    Where the capital is coming from (fundraising) 25
    Remuneration for the general partner 27

2. Process of a private equity transaction 30
    Approaching the target company 31
    Why a possible transaction should not be made public before the official announcement 35
    Why private equity funds are attractive to a target company 37
    Forms of the acquisition of company interests 41
    Examination of the target company 44
    Minority or majority investment 46
    Share or asset deal? 47
    Questions & Answers (Q&A) 48
    Site visit and management presentation 49
    Indicative offer 50
    Due Diligence 53

3. Forms of equity and debt financing 63
Types of equity 65
Types of debt 69
Further purchase price financing forms 76
Covenants 78
Structuring of the acquisition 81
SPA = Sales and purchase agreement 86

4. Post-investment phase 88
100-day Plan 89
Monitoring 90
Mentoring 91

5. Exit – The sale of the portfolio company 95
Sale to a strategic acquirer (also called trade sale) 95
Initial public offering (IPO) 96
Secondary buyout 96
Dual-track 97
Selecting the right exit channel 98

6. Leveraged buyout (LBO) valuation 99
Step 1: Creation of a pre-LBO model 102
Step 2: Creation of the transaction structure 107
Step 3: Creation of debt schedule and link with balance sheet, income statement, and cash flow statement 112
Step 4: Performing LBO analysis and return calculation .. 120

References 128

Literature recommendation for LBO valuations 131

Glossary 132

1 Introduction

Before the business model of private equity funds is explained, a practical example of a private equity transaction will be provided in this chapter.

<u>Hugo Boss AG acquired by Permira</u>
In 2007 the private equity fund Permira (based in London, U.K.) acquired approximately 80% of the Germany-based apparel company Hugo Boss AG.[1] After some great value-enhancing initiatives, Permira sold Hugo Boss AG in 2015. The transaction had a value of around EUR 5 billion. Permira was able to achieve a money multiple of 2.3 times the initial investment. The following key figures show how Hugo Boss AG developed after its acquisition by Permira:

- Number of employees grew from 9,123 in 2007 to 13,764 (growth of 51%) in 2015
- Number of stores grew from 287 in 2007 to 1,040 in 2015 (growth of 262%)
- EBITDA increased from EUR 272 million in 2007 to EUR 594 million in 2015 (growth of 118%)
- Total leverage (Net financial liabilities / EBITDA before special items) decreased from 0.6 in 2007 to 0.1 in 2015. (Note: In 2008, total leverage amounted to 2.1 due to the leveraged buyout; however, it decreased over the years)[2]

---

[1] For more details of the acquisition structure, see Chapter 3.
[2] Hugo Boss AG annual reports (2007 and 2015) and Permira Homepage

What is private equity and what is a private equity fund?

Besides private equity, there is public equity. Public equity is provided publicly by different types of investors when they buy stocks on stock exchanges. Private equity, on the other hand, is not provided publicly on stock exchanges, but privately or off-market. Many individual people invest in public equity (they buy stocks), however, in order to invest in private equity a certain amount of money is needed. Therefore, most people cannot invest directly into private equity funds. However, they can invest in funds which than invest in a private equity fund.

A private equity fund invests equity or equity-like capital in companies. The percentage stake the fund will invest in a company is different from transaction to transaction. However, to make operating changes to the portfolio company more easily, the fund is generally interested in acquiring a large stake. The acquired companies (or company stakes) are only held for a limited period of time, mostly between three and five years. The aim of the private equity fund is to increase the value of the companies and then sell them for high prices to achieve an attractive return.

Historic development of private equity

The discovery of America in 1492 by Christopher Columbus was only possible due to brave financiers who provided the money for this world-changing journey.

Many other similar white spots on the world map were discovered by private equity-like investors. For centuries investors have been providing capital and advice to economic projects to support the breakthrough of ideas. If the ideas become a success, the investors make a remarkable fortune.

However, the private equity investors as we know them nowadays only originated in the early 19th century. Wealthy individuals and private banks that invested in startups come close to today's definition of private equity. Many businesses which are today world-leading corporations were back then supported by private equity investors. These include companies like Rockefeller, AEG, and Phillips.

The first corporate entity that conforms to today's definition of private equity came into existence in 1946. The American Research and Development Corporation (ARD) was founded by three businessmen in Boston. However, besides the investment in the Digital Equipment Corporation (DEC), which they sold 14 years later for approximately 3,600 times the amount they had bought it for, the success of the firm was limited. The private equity industry was indirectly supported by the American government in 1957. The U.S. Internal Revenue Code made it possible for individual people to deduct capital losses from the tax if they had invested USD 25,000 in a startup company. With the introduction of the "Small Business Investment Act of 1958," the private equity industry got a further boost. The small business investment corporation was founded with this act. The purpose of the corporation was to support small businesses with capital and advice. The capital was provided by wealthy individuals.

In Germany, the first private equity firm was founded in 1960. Initially, the firm was quite like the traditional credit business since it mainly invested through a silent partnership. The aims were to improve the equity capital structure, to encourage innovation, and to create jobs.

Differences between private equity, venture capital, and hedge funds

The following graphic shows the first six phases of a company's lifecycle.

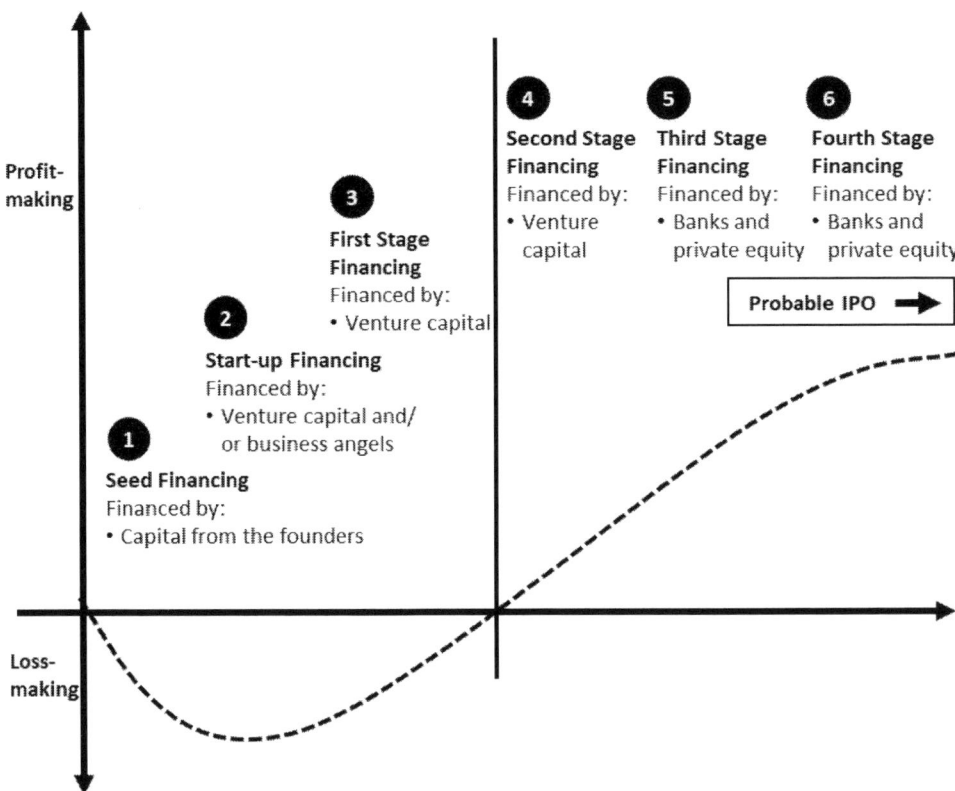

From the second until the fourth phase (from startup until second-stage financing), the company is regularly financed by venture capital funds. The classic private equity leveraged buyout fund invests in the subsequent phases (third- and fourth-stage financing). However, even after a company went public

(IPO = initial public offering), a private equity fund might invest in the company by buying its shares. Regularly, the private equity fund will then take the company private (public-to-private, Chapter 2).

The main difference from venture capital (VC) funds is that VC funds invest in relatively young companies (startups). As opposed to the leveraged buyout fund, a venture capital fund cannot acquire a company with a large amount of debt. This is because startup companies do not have enough cash flows to meet interest and debt repayments. The investment amount in a startup company is mostly also much smaller than an investment in an established company with a lot of tangible and intangible assets.

Since venture capital is also private equity, venture capital funds are often subsumed under the term "private equity." In this book, the term "private equity" exclusively means the classic private equity leveraged buyout fund.

<u>Differences between hedge funds and private equity funds</u>

Unlike private equity funds, hedge funds only invest in publicly listed companies (with few exceptions). They also do not acquire the whole company but only a few percentage. Moreover, most hedge funds do not actively push for operating or strategic changes in the company; they are passive investors. Nevertheless, there are some famous "active" investors such as Icahn Enterprises, founded by Carl Icahn.[3]

---

[3] http://www.ielp.com/; An example of an activist strategy: In 2013 and 2014, Carl Icahn bought around 0.9% of Apple Inc. stocks (worth about $3.6 billion) and told the Apple executive board that they should return some of the cash

The investment horizon of hedge funds is also much shorter than that of private equity funds. Depending on the hedge fund, stocks are bought and sold within seconds (the so-called high-frequency hedge funds) or a couple of months (rarely longer). Since hedge funds invest in public companies, they can also do short selling. In a short selling, a hedge fund borrows stocks from a stockholder (mostly banks who get a small fee for lending the stock) and sells them on the stock market. After a certain time, the hedge fund buys back the stocks on the stock market and returns them to the borrower. Thus, the hedge fund bets on a declining stock price. It hopes to sell the stock at a higher price before buying the stock back at a lower price.

A further difference lies in the fact that investors invest capital in a private equity fund for around 10–12 years. In a hedge fund, they invest the capital for a shorter time. In many hedge funds, investors can get their money back in a matter of months. That means that hedge funds remain under a permanent pressure to make profits. Otherwise, investors will invest the money elsewhere.

(which Apple had on the balance sheet) to investors. Icahn wrote a letter saying that Apple should do stock buyback in order to return some of the cash to investors. (When a company buys back some stocks from its investors, the remaining stocks will increase in value since there are fewer stocks left). In 2016, Icahn sold all of his Apple stocks. He said that he made with a 32-month holding period around $2 billion. http://www.marketwatch.com/story/carl-icahns-2-billion-apple-stake-was-a-prime-example-of-investment-inequality-2016-06-07. Active investors like Icahn also often make suggestions for strategic changes.

Private Equity - Greed for profit to the cost of employees?

Many private equity funds have received flak from the media. A notable example is Mitt Romney, who ran for president of the United States in 2012. He is a co-founder of the private equity firm Bain Capital (founded in 1984). During the presidential campaign, his opponents accused Romney of being a "predatory corporate raider" who does not mind cutting thousands of jobs if he can earn some money for himself.[4]

Allegedly, private equity funds buy a company, cut thousands of jobs, send production overseas to low-cost countries, and then sell the company after a few years for a large profit. Along the way, they apparently pay themselves high dividends and leave the company in bad conditions when they sell it. Additionally, they buy companies that are in financial trouble (financially distressed companies), and then they split the companies and sell the profitable parts. Allegedly, private equity funds are the reason why thousands of people lose their jobs along the way.

No doubt, not every transaction done by a private equity fund turns out to be a success for the company and for its employees. However, this also happens with companies that are not owned by a private equity fund. Often a strategy fails to work, or there is no overall strategy at all. This throws a company into difficult situations and can even lead to bankruptcy of the company.

The argument of private equity critics that private equity funds suck companies out through large dividend payments and leave them in bad conditions can be refuted. The private equity

---

[4] http://www.nytimes.com/2012/01/11/business/as-romney-campaign-advances-private-equity-becomes-part-of-the-debate.html

fund needs to sell the company after a few years since the fund matures and investors want their money back. If the company is in a bad condition during the sale process, interested buyers will not pay as much as the private equity fund needs to make a good return. They might even get less money than what they had bought the company for. The dividend payments (which the fund might pay itself during the holding period) will most likely be not enough to cancel out the low sale price. Therefore, the fund will work hard to increase the value of the company (e.g. through investments in profitable projects or/and through an improvement of the product portfolio). The dividend payments will therefore be only as high as it allows the company to invest and to grow.

As already mentioned, companies that are in financial trouble are quite often a target of private equity funds. These funds are often called "corporate raiders." They buy a distressed company and sell the valuable parts of the company to the highest bidder. Quite often a lot of employees lose their jobs during this sale process.

In the famous movie *Pretty Woman* (from 1990), featuring Julia Roberts and Richard Gere, Richard Gere plays a greedy investor. He wants to acquire a distressed company and sell the individual parts of the company to make a huge profit. He does not care that thousands of employees will lose their jobs along the way.

In the real world, the creditors (investors like banks) of the distressed company would mandate an investment bank to search for a new investor (e.g. private equity funds or operating corporations). Therefore, they would also talk to the Richard Gere-like "corporate raider." However, they will first of all talk to investors who believe in the future of the company and want to invest in the continuation of the company. This is because these investors can pay a higher price for the whole company. The whole company has generally a higher value than only the individual, separated parts can have. Moreover, since the investment bank's fee is a percentage (e.g. 2%) of the realized sale price, the investment bank is motivated to achieve a high price for the company and will want to find an investor who believes in the future of the company. This investor will invest in the company and thereby make sure that the jobs are saved (apart from some adjustments due to a restructuring plan).

Sometimes no investor is found who believes in the future of the company. Than the last resort is a corporate raider. If the company is not sold to a corporate raider, the company will be liquidated and all the employees will lose their jobs. The reason why creditors will likely sell the company to a corporate raider is that they can get quickly at least some of their money back (they will still make a loss). The corporate raider is experienced in selling individual parts (assets) of a company. He also knows who to contact to sell the assets. Furthermore, he is experienced in collecting the outstanding receivables of the company.

Overall, private equity funds can be considerably valuable for a company. They provide, for example, equity when the company wants to expand its business. Furthermore, they have a great network, extensive experience, and good connections with banks (for debt financing). The following chapters will investigate in greater detail how private equity can create value for a company. Nevertheless, every private equity fund should be checked (e.g. by investigating current and former portfolio companies) before business is done with the fund. This is because, as in all areas, in the private equity world also there are some "black sheep."

The private equity landscape

The following table shows 15 private equity funds which are some of the largest in the world.

Private Equity funds	Headquarter
Advent International	Boston, USA
Apax Partners	London, UK
Apollo Global Management	New York, USA
Bain Capital	Bosten, USA
Blackstone Group	New York, USA
Clayton Dubilier & Rice	New York, USA
CVC Capital Partners	Luxemburg City, LUX
General Atlantic	Connecticut, USA
Goldman Sachs Merchant Banking Division	New York, USA
Kohlberg Kravis Roberts (KKR)	New York, USA
Permira	London, UK
Silver Lake Partners	Menlo Park, USA
The Carlyle Group	Washington, D.C., USA
TPG Capital	San Francisco, USA
Warburg Pincus	New York, USA

From 2004 until 2016, the capital raised by private equity funds increased significantly. This can be seen in the chart "Globally raised capital by private equity funds." In 2016, the investments in private equity funds amounted to USD 589 billion. The chart shows that investments in private equity funds are correlated with the conditions of the stock markets. Until 2008 investments increased, while they decreased significantly in 2009 due to the financial crisis. This is because investments in private equity decrease when the "public equity market" is in a state of decline as well.

Globally raised capital by private equity funds (in billion USD)[5]

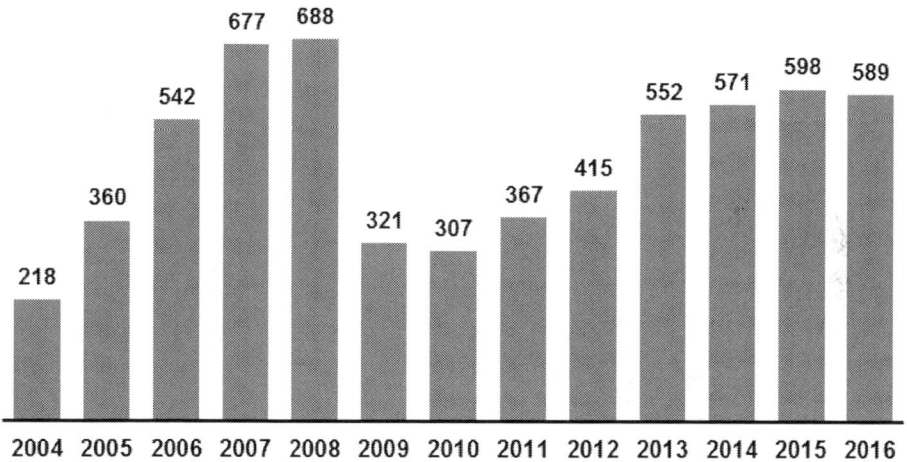

The assets under management by private equity funds (core private equity strategies encompassing buyout, venture capital,

---

[5] Bain & Company Global Private Equity Report 2017 includes all kinds of private equity funds (like venture capital, mezzanine, infrastructure, and distressed funds), not only buyout.

and other closely related strategies) amounted in June 2016 to USD 2.49 trillion (2,490,000,000,000).[6]

The largest market for private equity is the North American region. In 2014, North American funds raised around USD 290 billion. In comparison, European private equity funds raised USD 131 billion and Asian funds USD 55 billion in 2014.

---

[6] 2017 Preqin Global Private Equity and Venture Capital Report

Setup of the private equity environment

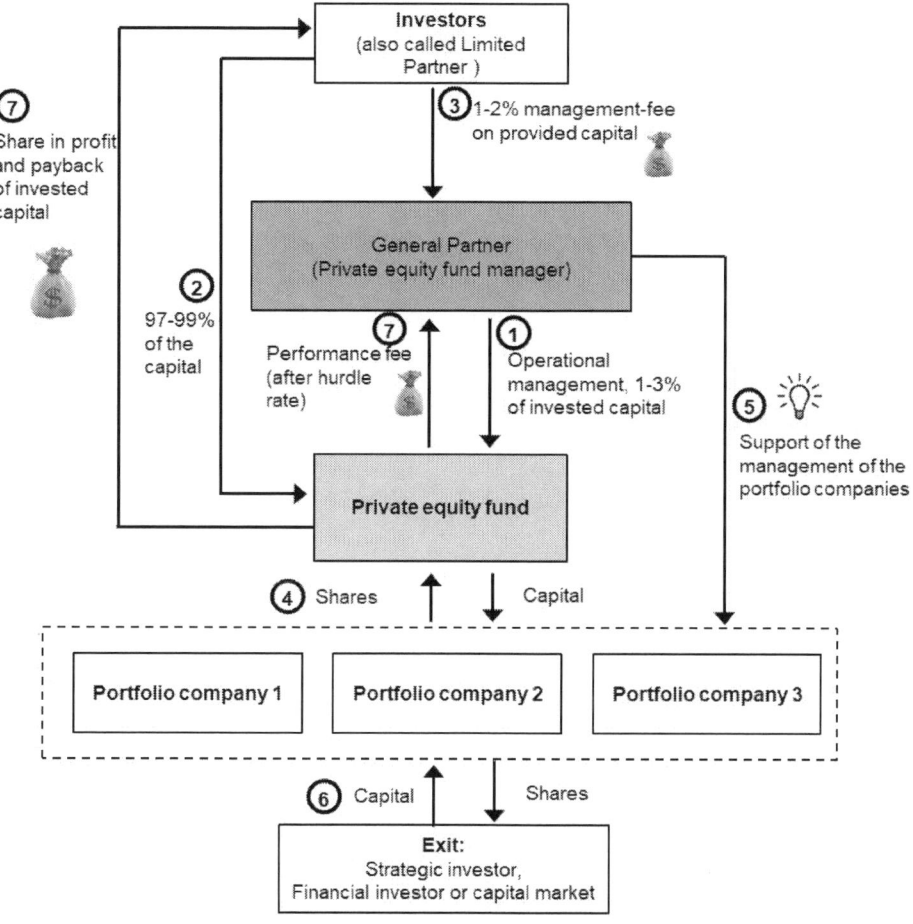

The above graphic shows how the private equity fund usually interacts with the individual players during the life of a private equity fund. Further explanations of the graphic refer to the circled numbers in the figure:

1) The general partner of the private equity fund is responsible for operating the fund. He is the fund manager when it

comes to a private equity firm or fund. The fund has a typical length of 10 years, with often a possible extension of three years. The general partner is responsible for fundraising, valuation and acquisition of target, planning of value-creation initiatives, and selling of the target (often with the help of consultants), among other things.

2) Most of the capital comes from limited partners who are institutional investors like insurance companies, pension funds, endowments, and wealthy individuals (more on that in the next section). At least 1% is provided by the general partner to have a higher alignment of interest. It is said that the general partner needs to have "some skin in the game."

3) The general partner charges a management fee of around 1–2% annually. This fee is not dependent on the success of the fund.

4) After due diligence from the general partner, the fund acquires the target company. Thus, the fund uses, in general, a substantial amount of debt, and a transaction is often executed with around 60–90% of debt. However, this is mainly the case in the U.S. Research about the European market suggests the level of debt is initially at 56.5–61.5% and is reduced during the holding period to 44.4–50% in European transactions.[7]

5) As mentioned in "1," the general partner often supports

---

[7] Achleitner, Braun, Engel, Figge, and Tappeiner (2010)

the target management with the planning of value creation initiatives, or advises them during the execution of an add-on acquisition (see Chapter 4 for more about value creation).

6) When a portfolio company gets sold to, for example, a public strategic investor, the private equity fund gets the realized proceeds. The money is already distributed when a company is sold, which means investors do not have to wait until the end of the life of a fund (around 10 years). The general partner returns the money to the investors and gets a share, as described in point "7.".

7) Often the so-called waterfall is agreed on and used to distribute the money. Thus, the limited partners will first of all receive their invested money back. Following this, the limited partners regularly get an annually preferred return (also called hurdle rate) of 8%. If after this there is still money left, the general partner gets his profit share (called carried interest or carry) of mostly about 20% of the capital left. The remaining 80% is for the limited partners.[8]

The typical career path in private equity

Private equity funds have very high expectations from their current and future employees. Considering the huge amount of money, the employees are responsible for, this is no surprise. In order to break into private equity, students need to graduate

---

[8] See, for example, Robinson and Sensoy (2013)

from top-tier universities (e.g. Harvard, Yale, Sandford, London School of Economics. The following chart shows a typical career path of an employee in a private equity fund:

```
Undergraduate School (Pre-MBA Candidates)
                    ↓
Summer analysts in a top-tier consulting or investment
                 banking program
                    ↓
Full-time Analyst program in consulting or investment banking
                    (1 – 3 years)
           ↓                              ↓
Graduate School (MBA)          Pre-MBA Associate
                                  (2 – 3 years)
           ↓                              ↓
Private Equity or Investment   Direct Promote to Senior
Banking Summer Associate       Associate (2 – 3 years)
           ↓                              ↓
Post-MBA Associate             Vice President (3 – 4 years)
   (2 – 3 years)
           ↓                              ↓
Vice President (3 – 4 years)   Director / Partner
           ↓
Director / Partner
```

Where the capital is coming from (fundraising)

The capital which is needed to acquire a target company comes from different types of investors. Most of it comes from institutional investors like insurance companies, pension funds, and banks. Further investors are large companies, governments, charities, as well as wealthy individuals. Besides, universities with large amounts of capital invest part of their wealth in private equity funds. For example, in 2016 the Harvard University invested 20% of their around USD 36 billion endowment fund in private equity funds (which includes venture capital).[9] The University of Notre Dame invested around 30% of its portfolio in private equity funds in 2014. The university states that, due to the returns from private equity, more students can be offered financial aid.[10]

The fundraising process (the process of collecting the fund's capital) can take, depending on the fund and the current market conditions, a different duration. The average fundraising duration in 2013 was 18.5 months, and in 2006 (an absolute boom year) the average duration was only 11.3 months.

Investors provide money for around 10 years. Apart from certain exceptions (which have to be agreed on in the contract), they cannot get access to the money before the end of the lifecycle of the fund (apart from the money which is distributed through dividends or exit proceeds). Consequently, the fundraising process takes some time. Investors check very carefully who receive the capital for such a long time. Therefore, private equity

---

[9] Harvard Management Company, Inc., Annual Endowment Report, September 2016
[10] http://www.pionline.com/article/20120820/PRINT/308209993/why-notre-dame-invests-in-private-equity

funds regularly use the so-called "placement agents" to help during the fundraising process (e.g. the search and talk to potential investors). The placement agents receive a success fee of around 1% of the successfully raised capital by the agents.

The target companies in which a private equity fund wants to invest generally remain unknown during the fundraising process (called blind pooling). Therefore, investors need to trust the fund's ability to find the right target companies. Convincing for the investors is often only the historical track record of the fund, which is an account of the past transactions and returns the private equity manager has achieved. A long reference list with many successful transactions is the mark of an experienced fund manager.

<u>Convincing investors without an extensive track record?</u>

A problem for young private equity funds is that they do not have an extensive track record. They cannot prove to investors that they have the ability to achieve great returns on their investments. Sometimes the fund managers worked in a private equity fund before they found their own and can at least use the investments they did in that fund as a starting point. Furthermore, new private equity funds can set up what is known as a pledge fund or uncommitted fund. In such a fund, investors do not provide the money for 10 or more years. Instead, the investors decide for every investment individually. This means that the fund managers have to convince the investors before every potential acquisition of a company. Only if the investors are convinced of the investment will they provide the money for the acquisition. Obviously, this means more work for the private equity fund and for the investors. However, this allows promising fund managers (without extensive track record) to prove their ability.

Remuneration for the general partner

Besides the profit the general partner (fund manager) makes through his own investments in the fund, he receives money through different components.

For once, as already mentioned, the general partner receives a fixed annual management fee of around 1–2% of the capital. Thus, this amount is regularly calculated on the *committed capital* in the first four to six years (called the investment period) and on the *invested capital* in the last four to six years (called the divestment period) of the fund's life. The management fee is used by the general partner to pay for the daily expenses of its company, e.g. personal expenses, office rent, insurance, and others. Furthermore, the general partner receives a performance fee. This fee is called carried interest (in short: carry). As already mentioned, the carry is paid out of the returns which are made with the investments (dividends and the profit received when a company is sold). For a calculation of the carried interest, see step 4 in Chapter *6, Leveraged buyout (LBO) valuation*. As the carried interest can make by far the largest part of the general partner's returns, he is highly motivated to make great investments in order to increase the carried interest. This means that the interest of the general partner and the investors are aligned.

Besides the management fee and the carried interest, there are transaction fees (also called deal or success fee) and monitoring fees. However, these fees are not paid by the investors but by the target companies (called portfolio companies after the acquisition). The transaction fee is paid when an acquisition is completed. The transaction fee for the general partner does not include fees which the target company has to pay for any transaction-related advice and service they receive from consultants, investment bankers, and lawyers.

In the study "Transaction and Monitoring Fees: On the Rebound?"[11] New York-headquartered law firm Dechert LLP investigated 143 transactions that had taken place between 2005 and 2010. The median transaction fee paid to the general partner was USD 5.1 million, which is 1% of the median transaction value.

The monitoring fee is charged to the portfolio company for regular consulting service provided by the general partner. Thus, it is often not said how many hours this consulting service will be provided. It is more a "when needed" consulting service. The median monitoring fee was USD 1.2 million per year in the transactions investigated by Dechert LLP. This is 1.42% of the EBITDA of the portfolio companies. In particular, the monitoring fee is often a subject of criticism. In the opinion of the critics, the monitoring fee is more a dividend which is paid even when the general partner is not providing any consulting work to the portfolio company. Tax experts are irritated by the fact that the monitoring fee is tax-deductible for the portfolio company, which would not be the case for a dividend.[12]

The criticism that the general partner is not providing any

---

[11] https://www.preqin.com/docs/reports/Dechert_Preqin_Transaction_and_Monitoring_Fees.pdf
[12] http://online.wsj.com/news/articles/SB10001424052702303743604579354870579844140

consulting work should be faced with the fact that the general partner has a huge interest in the improvement of the portfolio company. As already mentioned, a large amount of the general partner's compensation is the carried interest, which will be large when the portfolio company increases its value significantly. Very important is also the so-called free-riding principle. In this context, it means that the general partner gives advice to the portfolio company and thereby increases the value. However, other shareholders of the portfolio company (in case the private equity fund is not holding all 100% of the company's shares, which is often the case) also participate in the value enhancement although they do not do any work. When the general partner is paid a monitoring fee, the free-riding principle becomes void as the other shareholders indirectly (via the portfolio company) pay the general partner for its work.

Some general partners also charge portfolio companies fees for some or all of the following events: the completion of an add-on acquisition, the sale of a subsidiary, restructuring of the capital structure (e.g. issuing of a bond or equity capital increase), and the sale of the portfolio company. For all fees, it depends on the individual private equity fund if parts of the fees are distributed to the investors or if the general partner will keep all the proceeds.

2. Process of a private equity transaction

After the general partner has raised enough money from the investors, the actual work starts. The complete investment process, i.e. the acquisition, the value creation process, and last but not least the sale of the portfolio company will be discussed in the following section. The graphic "Typical steps of a leveraged buyout (LBO)" provides a general overview of the steps:

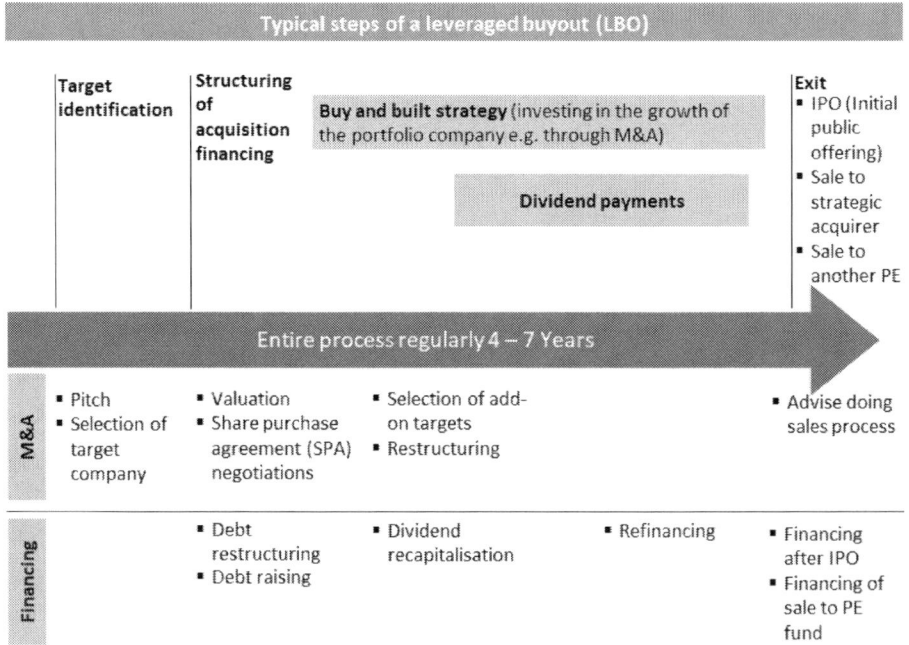

The steps of the process can be summarized as follows:

1. Approaching a suitable target company (in case the target company is already looking for a new investor, the

M&A advisor (investment banker) of the target company will contact the private equity fund).

2. Intensive due diligence of the target company as well as the industry of the target. During this step, the company will also be valuated with different valuation methods (discounted cash flow [DCF], multiple as well as leveraged buyout valuation).

3. Signing of the SPA (share purchase agreement) or APA (asset purchase agreement) and closing of the transaction.

4. Execution of a number of initiatives in order to increase the value of the portfolio company.

5. Sale of the portfolio company (exit).

Approaching the target company

In general, the private equity fund is approached by the M&A advisor of a company that is available for sale.

Private equity funds approach target companies as well, especially if they are looking for an add-on acquisition for a portfolio company. Through the combination of two companies, the private equity fund hopes to realize synergies. The approach is either done by the private equity fund itself or by an M&A advisor from the portfolio company. If the target company's owners are interested in a new investor, the sale process starts. Thus, the private equity fund prefers if the sale process is done via bilateral negotiation (exclusive negotiation) instead of an auction process (more than one bidder).

If the M&A advisor of a target company contacts a private equity fund, he will do that with an anonymized short profile (teaser) of the respective company. The teaser is a short version (of 2–4 pages) of the company. It includes a description of the business area the company is operating in as well as the products of the company. Furthermore, key financials are stated along with the main investment arguments. The aim of the teaser is to present the company in an attractive way in order to increase the interest in it and to make the potential investor want to have more information about the company. It is very important that the potential investor is unaware of the company the teaser is talking about. This is because the potential sale of a company (especially unlisted companies) should not be made public too soon for various reasons, which will be explained in in the next section. This means that the name of the company must not be written in the teaser. If the investor wants to have more information about the company (especially the name of the company and the company presentation), he needs to sign a non-disclosure agreement (NDA). This agreement states that the investor will not talk to third parties about the potential sale of the company. Following is a sample NDA:

PROJECT SAMPLE

Confidentiality Agreement regarding the examination of possible acquisition of a company acting in the example industries (the "Company") by sample acquirer (the "Interested Party")

*In the context of the evaluation of a possible purchase of shares in the Company (the **"Transaction"**) in a sale process organized by Example Advisor, (**"M&A Advisor"**) on behalf of the Seller, the Interested Party is interested in obtaining certain secret and confidential information with regard to the Company, including information about the business activities, the financial situation, the accounts, assets and liabilities (hereinafter: the **"Secret Information"**) from the Company. The term "Secret Information" shall also include the contents of any discussions on the Transaction and the fact that such discussions are taking place. Based on the foregoing, the Parties hereby agree as follows:*

1. By entering into this Agreement, the parties are obligated to ensure the confidentiality of the Secret Information made available to the Interested Party in connection with the evaluation of the Transaction. The Interested Party undertakes to maintain confidentiality with regard to the Secret Information and to make use of the Secret Information solely for purposes of evaluating the Transaction. The Interested Party will refrain from making available the Secret Information to any third party without the prior written consent by the Seller or by the Company.

2. The Interested Party may make available the Secret Information to employees and advisors engaged in the course of evaluating the Transaction and to banks financing the Transaction. The Interested Party shall be obliged to inform any such persons of the obligation of confidentiality existing under this Agreement prior to making available the Secret Information to any such party. The Interested Party shall guarantee the adherence of the aforementioned persons to the restrictions as set forth herein.

3. The obligation to keep secret and not to pass on information shall not apply with regard to information which

a) has otherwise become public;

b) has previously been given to the Interested Party by the Company or by its representatives on a non-confidential basis;

c) has been passed on to the Interested Party by any third party on a non-confidential basis, except where the third party has, to the knowledge of the Interested Party, acted in violation of any confidentiality agreement with the Seller or the Company.

4. The obligation of confidentiality shall not apply to the extent the Interested Party is obliged by mandatory law to disclose the Secret Information in legal, administrative, or any other proceedings. In these cases, the Company shall be informed upfront of any such obligation; such information must be accompanied by a legal opinion describing the obligation to disclose.

5. The Interested Party undertakes with regard to any documents, parts of documents, and copies of documents forwarded to him under this agreement and in his possession, to return, at the request of the Seller, any such documents to the Company or to destroy such documents and to confirm the destruction in writing to the Company. This shall not apply to the extent the Interested Party, banks, or advisors are under a statutory obligation to keep records or need to keep their own working papers for purposes of internal records, internal controlling or proof, it being understood that they shall be kept strictly confidential.

6. This Confidentiality Agreement shall not apply any obligation of the Company or the Seller to make available to the Interested Party any of the Confidential Information or any other information regarding the business of the Company. Neither the fact that the contemplated negotiations take place nor the disclosure of secret information in accordance with this Agreement shall constitute an obligation for either party to effect the Transaction or to enter into business relations with the other party.

7. The Seller, the M&A Advisor, and the Company do not assume any explicit or implied warranty or liability whatsoever for the accuracy or completeness of the information; any such liability of the Seller, the M&A Advisor, or the Company shall be excluded except to the extent express warranties, if any, shall be given by the Seller in the definitive purchase agreement. The extent to which the liability for the Seller under such representations and warranties shall be excluded if deviations from such representations and warranties result from information which has been

disclosed to the Interested Party by Seller or the Company, shall be governed by the definitive purchase agreement.

8. The Interested Party shall not directly contact any employees or members of the management of the Company without the prior written consent of the M&A Advisor. Any contact with the Company shall be managed exclusively through the M&A Advisor. During the examination and within a period of two years after the end of the examination, the Interested Party and its affiliates shall be prohibited from influencing or attempting to influence any employees or members of the management of the Company with regard to any employment or engagement as advisor for the Interested Party or any of its affiliates. The Interested Party shall be responsible for compliance with this provision by its affiliates.

9. This Agreement shall remain in effect through December 31, 2020.

10. This Agreement shall be subject to the laws of the United States of America.

11. Any disputes under this Agreement shall be subject to the exclusive jurisdiction of the courts of New York City.

_____   _____

Date   *Interested Party*

This is a sample NDA and can be different in practice. Sometimes, the parties agree on different, individual NDAs through negotiations. It is important that the NDA states that the investor will treat the information as confidential.

Why a possible transaction should not be made public before the official announcement

The M&A advisor always uses code names for a sale project. Example code names for a project are "Project Phoenix" or

"Project Mars."[13] These are used to hide the real company name during the first approach of an investor. What is more, during further conversations and negotiations, a code name is always helpful. If an M&A advisor wants to talk to the designated representative of a potential investor (for strategic or operating investors, this is regularly the business development department, or in large companies the M&A department) and only reaches a colleague of her, who should not know about the transaction, it is helpful to have a code name. The M&A advisor can explain to the person the reason for the call without having to divulge the name of the company that is up for sale.

In case a transaction is made public before the announcement, this regularly has negative consequences for many areas.[14] Employees of the company could, for example, think that they will lose their job after the transaction. In particular, good employees will likely find a new job relatively quick and might leave the company before it is sold to a new investor even when the employees would most likely not have lost their jobs after the transaction. Besides, if the employees would not leave the company, they might apply to other companies and approach their current employer with higher salary demands.

What is more, suppliers could think that the company is looking for an investor because it is in financial distress. In the worst case, the suppliers would not supply any goods to the company

---

[13] https://blogs.intralinks.com/2014/12/whats-ma-project-name/
[14] This is especially true for companies which are not listed on a stock exchange (private companies). This is because the financial situation of these companies cannot be as easily evaluated as those of listed companies (public companies). This is due to the fact that private companies do not provide as much information about their financial situation as public companies do.

without getting paid in advance. This would mean that the company has to pay for the goods before actually getting them, which could have considerable negative consequences.

Customers could also think that the company is in financial distress. The problem here is that customers could believe that the company will not meet their warranty promises on the products, which could lead to a decrease in the number of customers.

Why private equity funds are attractive to a target company

Why do the owners of a company want to sell some or all shares of their company to a private equity fund? There are some reasons for this, which will be explained in the following section.

Growth financing

If a company wants to grow its business (e.g. by developing new products or entering new geographic), it regularly needs some capital for the respective investments. Quite often the cash flow (or the internal financing capability) of the company is not sufficient to finance the investments. Traditional banks might not be the right capital providers as the investment might be too risky for them. Private equity funds can provide the right solution. As the investment will increase the value of the company, assuming it pays off both the "old" owner and the private equity fund, this can result in an attractive return.

An example of such a growth financing is the company Amor (German retailer of jewelry). In 2010, the private equity fund 3i Group (fund based in London, U.K.) bought a minority share of the company and supported its international expansion actively. In the years 3i Group was invested in Amor (from 2010 until 2016), the company's EBITDA increased by around 60%. With the sale of the company, 3i Group realized a money multiple of around 2.5 times (which means that the private equity fund more than doubled the initial investment. More on money multiple in Chapter 6. Leveraged buyout (LBO) valuation, Step 4.).[15]

Public-to-private

Public-to-private means that an investor (generally it does not need to be a private equity fund) is acquiring a publicly traded company and is delisting the company (taking it private) from the stock exchange. This is also done by private equity funds. A famous example of such a public-to-private transaction is the company Dell and the private equity fund Silver Lake. In 2013, Silver Lake, along with Dell founder Michael Dell, bought all outstanding stocks of Dell and took the company private. This opportunity often arises when the company is not doing well, and deep strategic changes are needed to make the company great again. Dell had also some profitability problems, especially because they did not adapt quickly enough to the rise of the mobile and cloud computing business. As a private company, without the pressure on short-term earnings, it was easier for Michael Dell (who is CEO of Dell) and Silver Lake to develop a

---

[15] http://www.3i.com/~/media/Files/G/Group-3i/documents/case-studies/amor.pdf

long-term strategy which makes Dell profitable again. For example, a member of the Dell executive board told Bloomberg that the decisions are now made much quicker and that they are not distracted by investor meetings or analyst conference calls.[16]

Carve-out

When a company sells parts of its business (a business unit or a subsidiary) to new investors, it is called a carve-out. The parent company thus regularly sells interests of the subsidiary to the new investors. The control is often still with the parent company. A carve-out makes sense when the subsidiary is deeply integrated in the parent's operations; however, the plan is to separate the two companies eventually. These transactions make sense for a private equity fund if they see value creation opportunities for the subsidiary as a standalone company.

An example of such a carve-out is the transaction between KKR (one of the largest private equity firms in the world) and Airbus. In February 2017, Airbus completed the carve-out of its Germany-based defense electronic business (enterprise value of approx. EUR 1.1 billion). They sold 74,9% of the business to KKR, which will rename it "Hensoldt."[17]

Turnaround (restructuring)

If a company is in financial distressed new equity investments from private equity funds are a possible solution. Specialized private equity funds have a lot of experience in restructuring a

---

[16] http://www.bloomberg.com/news/articles/2014-11-06/dell-silver-lake-said-to-reap-90-gain-a-year-after-lbo
[17] http://www.airbusgroup.com/int/en/news-media/press-releases/Airbus-Group/Financial_Communication/2017/02/DefenceElectronicsClosing.html

company. They know how to restructure the balance sheet in order to return to profitability. What is more, they often will negotiate better terms with the financing banks which will ease the financial burden. In addition, consultants can be hired to assist in the restructuring process. This would not be possible without the equity investment of the private equity fund as the consultants probably could not be paid.

The private equity fund Sun Capital Partners (U.S.-based private equity fund with around USD 9 billion under management) often invests in companies with declining profitability. In 2010, Sun Capital acquired Captain D's Seafood Kitchen (U.S.-based Casual Seafood Chain), which had suffered several years of declining store sales. After the acquisition, Sun Capital strengthened the management team of Captain D, implemented new financial controls and a robust procurement process, and improved labor management. Furthermore, the customer's experience was enhanced by a new restaurant design, improved food quality, etc. This resulted in 27 consecutive periods of system-wide comparable sales growth.[18]

Sale due to retirement

Another reason why company owners might want to sell their company to a private equity fund is their age. If they are also managing their company and want to retire, private equity funds can be a solution. Through the sale of the company, they will likely get enough money to enjoy retirement. It is advisable for company owners to seek contact to a fund some years before

---

[18] https://www.suncappart.com/affiliate-of-sun-capital-partners-inc-enters-into-definitive-agreement-to-sell-captain-ds-seafood-restaurant/

the retirement. Often a company that is managed by the owner is tailored to the owner, which can make it hard to transfer the management to a new owner. The private equity fund will therefore appreciate if the company owner is available for a smooth transition of the company to the fund.

Forms of the acquisition of company interests

Management buyout (MBO)

The management buyout is a company acquisition done by the management of that company. Since the management has regularly not enough capital to acquire the company, a private equity fund will invest along the management and provide most of the capital. The management will receive a small percentage (mostly up to 20% via sweet equity; more information about sweet equity in Chapter 3) of the company's equity. A big advantage of a management buyout is that the management already knows the company they are acquiring. After the acquisition, it is highly motivated to improve the company as it is deeply involved in the success of the company. However, it will also lose a lot of money if the company does not grow positively.

For the old owner of the company, a management buyout makes sense if, for example, they want to retire and do not have offspring to manage the company. Furthermore, a management buyout makes sense in case of a carve-out. Thereafter, the management of the old subsidiary will form a new company and continue to manage it with the new support of the private equity fund.

Management buy-in (MBI)

In a management buy-in, an external management buys a company they did not work for in the past. This is different from the management buyout where the acquiring management has already worked for the company. This form of acquisition is used when the current management of the company fails to perform well. However, also when a family-owned company intends to sell the company, this form might be a solution. An obvious danger or uncertainty is that the new management might not be right for the company. The new management might, for example, not fit in the culture and does not get along with the employees. However, the responsibility of the private equity fund is to ensure that the new management is suitable for the company. If it is not suitable, then the fund needs to realize this quickly and change the management accordingly.

Leveraged buyout (LBO)

The needed capital for a company investment does not only come from the private equity fund in the form of equity. Frequently, the private equity fund will also raise debt from banks or other investors (e.g. private debt funds) to finance the acquisition. The debt will be put on the balance sheet of the target company, which means that the company will indirectly pay for the acquisition. Therefore, the private equity fund makes use of the leverage effect[19]. The United States Bank Authorities call for

---

[19] The leverage effect is the effect that the debt has on the equity return. When

a leveraged buyout when the percentages of debt used for the buyout is more than 50% of the overall capital used. The interest and the repayments are paid with the cash flow of the target company and sometimes with the proceeds of the sale of some parts of the business that do not fit in the business model any longer. Besides the leverage effect, leveraged buyout has further advantages. The interest payments go through the profit and loss statement as expenses, meaning that they decrease the income taxes the company has to pay. This tax deduction is called "Tax Shield." This is also one of the reasons why debt is cheaper than equity. It should be noted that in some countries (such as Germany) the tax-deductibility of interest payments is limited to a certain threshold. In Germany, the deductibility is limited to the balance of interest payable and interest receivable. If the balance is negative (i.e. more interest was paid than received), then deductibility is limited to 30% of the taxable EBITDA. This can be avoided by creating a taxable entity (for more information about taxable entities, see Chapter 3).

Furthermore, the management of the target company needs to pay the interest first before spending the cash flow on any projects. Therefore, the management cannot be wasteful with the cash flows which is reducing the agency problem. This is also called the debt control hypothesis.

In a leveraged buyout, a special valuation method is used which is explained with a case study in Chapter 6.

---

the cost of debt (e.g. 5%) is lower than the return on investment (e.g. 15% because the company receives a return of 15% on the debt and equity invested), an increase in the amount of debt can increase the equity return.

Examination of the target company

After the private equity fund signed the non-disclosure agreement (NDA) it will receive further information about the target company.

One part of the information will regularly be a comprehensive "fact book" in the form of PowerPoint slides provided by the M&A advisor of the target company. This fact book is also often called information memorandum. This memorandum provides the private equity fund with information about the industry, the main competitors, the main suppliers as well as the products of the company. Further information includes the organization, the strategy, as well as the financial situation (including historical, current, and projected balance sheet; profit and loss calculation; and cash flow statement) of the company. Using the information (and its own research), the private equity fund should be able to make a first indicative offer (more on the indicative offer later).

In addition to the information memorandum, the private equity fund will receive a process letter. This letter provides the fund with information about the next steps in the acquisition process. It states until when the indicative offer should be made to be considered in the next steps. Furthermore, it states which information the private equity fund needs to include in the indicative offer.

To create the indicative offer, the private equity fund generally uses the following information:

- Information memorandum (in the form of comprehensive PowerPoint slides)
- Industry experts
- Questions they ask the target company (Q&A)

- Site visit and management presentation (not always <u>before</u> the indicative offer)

Industry experts

In order to understand and examine the target company in the best possible way, private equity funds regularly have a network of industry experts which provide them with advice. These industry experts have worked for many years in leading positions and have deep insights into the respective industry. Moreover, for both political and regulatory issues, private equity funds use experts. The private equity firm Carlyle Group (one of the largest private equity funds in the U.S.) currently has 34 industry experts as advisers. One of these experts is Charles O. Rossotti, who specializes in the Technology & Business Services industry. He has worked many years in the industry and also found a company in this field. He is on the board of directors of Coalfire, ECi Software, LDiscovery, and Novetta, which are all portfolio companies of Carlyle. Furthermore, he is on the board of directors of Booz Allen Hamilton and Quorum Management Solutions, which are former Carlyle portfolio companies.[20]

The experts are also often available for advice even after the acquisition. Sometimes they even take a management position in the target company to improve the business. Furthermore, a private equity fund will do its own research about the target company and the industry. The fund will therefore never solely rely on the information memorandum.

Depending on how the M&A advisor has planned the sale

---

[20] https://www.carlyle.com/about-carlyle/team/charles-o-rossotti

process, the private equity fund and other interested parties get more or less information before the indicative offer is due. It is possible that the M&A advisor is only sharing the information memorandum before the indicative offer. This especially means that the private equity fund cannot ask any questions to the management of the target company prior to making the indicative offer.

Minority or majority investment

For a private equity fund, it makes quite a difference if a company owner wants to sell a minority or a majority share of his company. Most private equity funds prefer to invest in a majority share. This is because the fund can enforce their strategic changes easier when they hold more voting rights (since they hold the minority). Furthermore, the timing for the exit is more in the hands of the fund and is crucial for the fund. Some funds do not even look at an investment opportunity if it is a minority investment.

However, many funds also invest in minority opportunities since these investments have some advantages:
- The cost-intensive auction process which is often used in buyouts (sale of majority shares) can sometimes be avoided.
- Debt financing is not endangered by the so-called chance of-control clauses[21] from debt or supplier contracts or alike.

---

[21] A change of control clause (also known as change of control) is a provision

- Since the majority of the shares stay with the previous company owner, it is certain that the owner still believes in the company and is highly motivated to further improve it.
- A takeover of the remaining shares can be prepared and executed after some time. The private equity fund gets to know the company better before fully taking it over while also avoiding an expensive auction process for the remaining shares.

Share or asset deal?

Legally, it is interesting for the fund if the acquisition is done via a share or an asset deal.

Share deal

In a share deal, the shares of the company are bought. Symbolically, this is a certificate which proves that the acquirer owns the company. In a share deal, the acquirer buys all assets and liabilities from the previous owner. Since the acquirer also buys liability risks (some of which the acquirer might not even know about during the acquisition), certain accountability agreements (guaranties of the seller) are often necessary. A share deal has the

---

in a contract that gives a party (e.g. in a debt contract the debt provider) certain rights (e.g. termination of debt contract) in the event of a change in ownership of the other party to the agreement (e.g. the company which is provided with the debt). A change of control might be triggered, for example, when more than 50% of stocks of the respective company are sold.
https://uk.practicallaw.thomsonreuters.com/0-382-3325?originationContext=document&transitionType=DocumentItem&contextData=(sc.Default)&firstPage=true&bhcp=1

advantage that the share purchase agreement is often leaner than the agreement in an asset deal. A share deal is used when a company is sold which is in a good condition and not in financial distress.

Asset deal

In an asset deal, all rights and contracts are sold and transferred individually. The advantage is that every item is examined individually, and the acquirer knows exactly what he is buying. An obvious disadvantage of the asset deal is that the asset purchase agreement is quite extensive, since every item which is sold needs to be included in the contract. This includes all work, contractual, and legal relationships of the respective assets. An asset deal is regularly done when the company is in financial distress. This allows the acquirer, for example, to avoid buying all work contracts (laying off people is often used as the first step to restructuring a company). Furthermore, it reduces liability risks.

Questions & Answers (Q&A)

Many M&A advisers allow interested buyers to ask a limited number of questions to the management of the target company even before the initial offer. If they do not allow this before the initial offer, it will definitely be after the evaluation of the initial offers, when some bidder (due to low initial offers or lost interest) left the sale process. The Q&A process is a part of the due diligence process. It is important to document during the whole sale process which information is exchanged. This is done to prevent legal disputes after the acquisition. This documentation is done via virtual data rooms where all information is stored. A data room is like a cloud platform with high security standards in order to prevent unauthorized people from getting access to the information. Authorized users only need an internet connection to access the information stored in the data room. This has the obvious advantage that the potential acquirer does not need to go to the company's site to see the information. Another major advantage is that it is automatically documented which documents the potential acquirer received and saw. This can prevent law disputes in case the acquirer thinks he did not receive important information. Before the advent of the internet, this data room used to be a physical room in which all information was stored in innumerable physical files. An employee of the M&A advisor had to be in the room to record which documents the interested acquirer was seeing. Obviously, only one interested acquirer at a time was allowed in the room. Thanks to the internet, this process is much more efficient nowadays.

The Q&A process is also done via the data room. The interested acquirer can raise the questions there and also receives the answers via the data room. This allows reducing the number of emails to be sent, and thoroughly documenting the questions and answers.

Site visit and management presentation

In a site visit, the interested acquirer visits the company's site and meets with the management. This site visit generally includes a management presentation, whereby the management introduces the company as well as the strategy of the company. If there are many interested parties, a site visit and management presentation would not be reasonable due to the organizational effort (for every interested party an individual meeting needs to be arranged). This is also because the management is supposed to run the company and not hold countless meetings with potential acquirers. Hence, a site visit and management presentation are often done after the initial offer. The number of interested parties commonly decreases after the initial offer, because some parties offer an extremely low acquisition price or do not make any initial bid at all (since they are not interested anymore).

Indicative offer

An example indicative offer is shown in the following. In practice, the indicative offers obviously variate.

<u>Indicative offer for the acquisition of SAMPLE Group</u>

With this letter, we want to present our indicative offer to acquire the SAMPLE Group. The total purchase price we offer is:

USD 95,000,000 (In words: Ninety-five million USD)

The purchase price refers to the acquisition of all shares of the following corporations ("SAMPLE Group") in the form of a share deal:
- Sample Corporation A (100% of all shares)
- Sample Corporation B (100% of all shares)

This indicative offer is not binding, nor does it depend on

further company analyses and negotiations. An acquisition is based on the following assumptions:

- Talks and agreement with banks about the future conditions of the existing liabilities in the amount of USD 45,387,000 (as of: 31.12.2017)
- Plausibility check of the needed working capital under considerations of the payment procedure with customers and suppliers
- Examination of the business plan for the years 2018–2019, especially additional short- and long-term investments, current orders in hand, as well as plausibility check of the revenue growth
- Talks with the current management about the continuation concept and their role in the company
- Talks with the main customers about the continuation of the business relations with the SAMPLE Group
- Tax and legal examination for possible off-balance liabilities and contingent liabilities

After a first meeting with the management, we would plan further due diligence (DD) requirements with you. It is assumed that the seller will cooperate fully, and that it will neither wittingly or unwittingly withhold or slow down the provision of information.

Continuation concept

Our continuation concept includes the following strategic milestones:

- We see growth potential internationally: Owing to our

connections to India (Head of Sales Adidas in New Delhi) and Russia, we see a major focus on these countries for our expansion to Eastern Europe and Asia.

- Stabilization of the customer relations and core processes at the headquarters with a focus on development and sales

- Adjustments of the whole performance and the product portfolio to the strength of the company as well as the economic situation with a focus on:

  - Identification of deficient projects (if present)

  - Replacement of certain suppliers for simple components trough cheaper sources in low cost countries (under the condition of good reference by customers)

  - Supply chain and buy and build optimization

  - Improvement of production processes and general process optimization

  - Increasing the contribution per employee

  - The Six Sigma program

- Stabilization of the customer relations and strategic orientation on the core competences

- Examination of the risk management in contracts, and supplier and customer relationships

Financing of the Transaction

The transaction is financed by equity and debt. Therefore, we still need the confirmations by banks and other debt providers with which we are in negotiations. For us, as well as the banks and the debt providers, the acquisition is only dependent on the upcoming due diligence, which needs to confirm the reasonableness of the purchase price and the purchase agreement.

Time frame

The plan is to complete the transaction by April 30, 2018. The full corporation of the seller is necessary in order to accomplish this. In particular, no information can be withheld. Complete access to customer and supplier documents, as well as talks and data for the validation of the provided documents, is assured to us. We assume that site visits, management presentations, and meetings can be arranged shortly. We are happy if you could provide us with the respective date proposals.

Other

We reserve the right to withdraw from this initial offer in the following process without citing any reasons and paying any costs, or being responsible for any claim of damage.
We are available for any questions.
Kind regards,
Max Mayer,
CEO of Private Capital Group

Due Diligence

If the company seller accepts the indicative offer (the purchase price and other elements need to be acceptable to the seller), then the due diligence process starts for the private equity fund. During due diligence, the private equity fund investigates the company in great detail. All important legal contracts and alike (legal due diligence) are investigated as well as all tax (tax due diligence), financial (financial due diligence), and commercial (commercial due diligence) matters are investigated in great detail. Private equity funds often hire special consultants to help with the due diligence process.

Following is a sample due diligence list about which information the private equity fund will seek from the seller. Some information will need to be researched by the consulting firms. In general, the private equity fund should not only rely on the information provided by the seller.

Sample Due Diligence List

I. Financial Information *(Financial DD)*
A. Annual and quarterly financial information for the past five years (years might vary)
1. Income statements, balance sheets, cash flows, and footnotes
2. Planned versus actual results
3. Management financial reports
4. Breakdown of sales and gross profits by:
   a. Product type
   b. Channel
   c. Geography
5. Current backlog by customer (if any)
6. Accounts receivable aging schedule

B. Financial Projections

1. Quarterly financial projections for the next three fiscal years *(years might vary)*
   a. Revenue by product type, customers, and channel
   b. Full income statements, balance sheets, cash flow statements
2. Major growth drivers and prospects
3. Risks attendant to foreign operations (e.g., exchange rate fluctuation, government instability)
4. Industry and company pricing policies
5. Economic assumptions underlying projections (different scenarios based on price and market fluctuations)
6. Explanation of projected capital expenditures, depreciation, and working capital arrangements
7. External financing arrangement assumption

C. Capital Structure

1. Current shares outstanding
2. List of all stockholders with shareholdings, options, warrants, or notes
3. Schedule of all options, warrants, rights, and any other potentially dilutive securities with exercise prices and vesting provisions.
4. Summary of all debt instruments/bank lines with key terms and conditions
5. Off balance sheet liabilities

D. Other financial information *(Financial/tax DD)*

1. Summary of current federal, state and foreign tax positions, including net operating loss carry forward
2. Discuss general accounting policies (revenue recognition,

etc.)

3. Schedule of financing history for equity, warrants, and debt (date, investors, dollar investment,

percentage ownership, implied valuation and current basis for each round)

II. Products *(Commercial DD)*
A. Description of each product
1. Major customers and applications
2. Historical and projected growth rates
3. Market share
4. Speed and nature of technological change
5. Timing of new products, product enhancements
6. Cost structure and profitability

III. Customer Information
A. List of top 10 customers for the past three fiscal years and current year-to-date by application *(number of customers and years might vary)* (name, contact name, address, phone number, product(s) owned, and timing of purchase(s))
B. List of strategic relationships
(name, contact name, phone number, revenue contribution, marketing agreements)
C. Revenue by customer
(name, contact name, phone number for any accounting for 5% or more of revenue) *(percentages might vary)*
D. Brief description of any significant relationships severed within the last two years.
(name, contact name, phone number)

E. List of top 5 suppliers for the past three fiscal years and current year-to-date with contact information *(number of suppliers and years might vary)*
(name, contact name, phone number, purchase amounts, supplier agreements)

IV. Competition

A. Description of the competitive landscape within each market segment including:

1. Market position and related strengths and weaknesses as perceived in the market place
2. Basis of competition (e.g. price, service, technology, distribution)

V. Marketing, Sales, and Distribution

A. Strategy and implementation

1. Discussion of domestic and international distribution channels
2. Positioning of the Company and its products
3. Marketing opportunities/marketing risks
4. Description of marketing programs and examples of recent marketing/product/public
relations/media information on the Company

B. Major Customers

1. Status and trends of relationships
2. Prospects for future growth and development
3. Pipeline analysis

C. Principal avenues for generating new business

D. Sales force productivity model

1. Compensation
2. Quota Average
3. Sales Cycle
4. Plan for New Hires

E. Ability to implement marketing plan with current and projected budgets

VI. Research and Development
A. Description of R&D organization
1. Strategy
2. Key Personnel
3. Major Activities

B. New Product Pipeline
1. Status and Timing
2. Cost of Development
3. Critical Technology Necessary for Implementation
4. Risks

VII. Management and Personnel *(Human research DD)*
A. Organization Chart
B. Historical and projected headcount by function and location
C. Summary biographies of senior management, including employment history, age, service with the Company, years in current position
D. Compensation arrangements
1. Copies (or summaries) of key employment agreements
2. Benefit plans

E. Discussion of incentive stock plans

F. Significant employee relations problems, past or present

G. Personnel Turnover

1. Data for the last two years
2. Benefit plans

VIII. Legal and Related Matters *(Legal DD)*

A. Pending lawsuits against the Company

(detail on claimant, claimed damages, brief history, status, anticipated outcome, and name of the Company's counsel)

B. Pending lawsuits initiated by Company

(details on defendant, claimed damages, brief history, status, anticipated outcome, and name of the Company's counsel)

C. Description of environmental and employee safety issues and liabilities

1. Safety precautions
2. New regulations and their consequences

D. List of material patents, copyrights, licenses, and trademarks

(issued and pending)

E. Summary of insurance coverage/any material exposures

F. Summary of material contacts

G. History of SEC or other regulatory agency problem, if any

Due diligence is done with the help of specialized consultants. For legal due diligence, law firms are hired. For tax due diligence, often large auditing firms like Deloitte, EY, KPMG, and PwC are roped in. The commercial due diligence is often done by large strategy consultants like Bain & Company, Boston Consulting Group (BCG) or McKinsey. However, often it makes sense for the private equity firm to hire special consultants for a certain industry. If a private equity fund wants to acquire a company in the defense industry, it is feasible to hire a strategy consulting firm that is specialized in this field.

The cost of due diligence should not be underestimated. They can easily make up to 30–50% of the transaction costs. Often private equity firms therefore agree with the seller on breakup fees. Should the transaction fail because of the seller than the private equity fund can bill the target company with the agreed breakup fee.

Exit Scenario

The main difference between a strategic investor[22] and a private equity fund that is doing due diligence is that the private equity fund needs to think about the exit strategy already during the due diligence process. This is because the private equity fund needs to sell the company after a few years. The strategic investor, on the other hand, generally wants to be invested for a much longer time. The exit can be done in different ways, which will be explained in more detail in Chapter 5.

---

[22] A strategic investor is a company that acquires another company for strategic reasons. Strategic reasons can be to gain excess to a new market in terms of the product (a product the target company has which would be great for the current customers), customer (contacts and relationships with customers of the target companies), or geographical location (if the target is, for example, strong in China, which the company wants to enter). Another reason is the economy of scale (e.g. increased purchase power due to higher volumes of purchase).

Management team after the transaction

In addition, extremely important for the private equity fund is the selection of the right operating management of the target company. Only in very few cases the private equity fund does the operative management and therefore regularly needs to hire a management team.[23] In the form of a management buyout, where the current management of the target stays as the management, the fund does not need to look for a new management. However, it needs to ensure that the management is qualified, which will be checked during due diligence. The motivation for the management is that they get a stake in the company and are thus directly financially affected by the performance of the company (which largely depends on their own performance).

Motivation of the seller

In meetings with the current owner of the company, the private equity fund should find out the motivation for the sale. If the fund estimates that the owner no longer believes in the business model of the company, the fund should take caution. The fund will likely find out if the business model has a future or not. If the business model needs to be adjusted in order to have a growing future, the fund needs to ensure that they have the skills (together with the management) to do this.

Cash flow

Besides paying the purchase price, a private equity fund often does not want to invest a lot of money in a company. The capital

---

[23] Distressed private equity funds sometimes do the management themselves and act as an interim manager until the company is in a better state and until they found the right management.

for the main investments (to improve the company) the private equity fund wants the company to do, need to come from the company itself. Hence, the fund will check if the company has high enough cash flows to finance any future investments. Moreover, the creditworthiness of the company will be checked so that the company can raise debt for investments. The private equity fund will finance the acquisition with both equity and debt. The debt will be put on the balance sheet of the company, meaning that it has to pay the interest and the repayments. The cash flow needs to be high enough to meet these payments. How much debt the cash flow can deal with is analyzed in Chapter 6. *Leveraged buyout (LBO) valuation.*

3. Forms of equity and debt financing

The necessary capital for the purchase price is, as already mentioned, a part equity and a part debt. Some private equity funds use financial engineering. The meaning of financial engineering is that one looks for innovative financing solutions with the use of different traditional financial products. Owing to the complexity and the different forms of such engineering, it will not form part of the following discussion. The following graphic shows possible capital sources of a buyout transaction, the *New corp.* thereby represents the acquisition corporation:

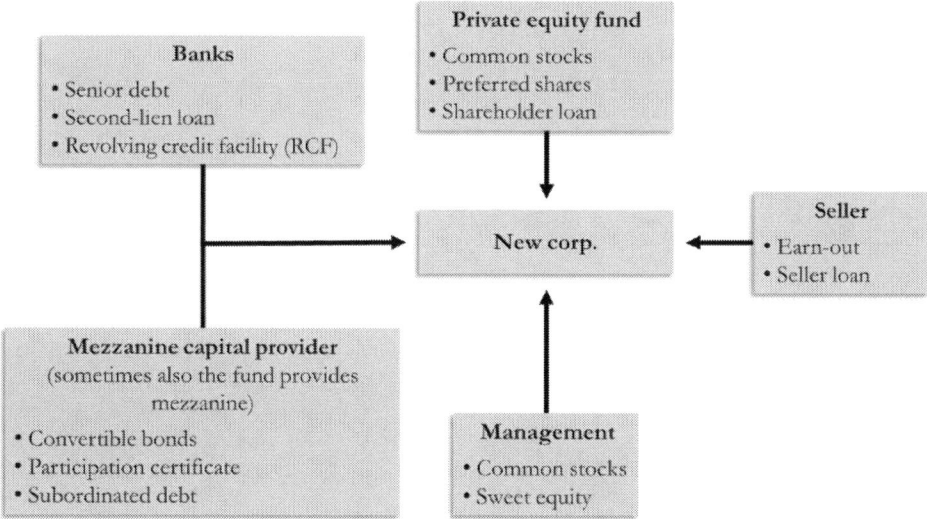

Subsequently, different capital sources are explained. First of all, the differences between equity and debt are explained in the following table:

Differences between equity and debt

	Equity	Debt
Legal relationship	Ownership	Debt obligation
Liability / Responsibility	Depending on the legal form the equity owner is hold responsible with all his wealth (including the private wealth) however, at least with his investment.	The debt holder is not responsible for any losses. In case of insolvency he is served before the equity holder
Return / Income	The shareholder gets a share of the profit in relation to its share in the company. However, if the company is losing money he is not getting anything and his shares decrease in value.	Get interests on the provided debt,, even if the company is making losses he has the right to receive interests
Participation	Entitled to participate in the company's decision	No participation right
Maturity	Equity is principally perpetual	Debt is provided for a limited period of time
Taxation (in the view of the company)	Dividends and other equity distributions are generally not tax deductible	Debt interest payments are generally tax deductible
Motivation	Equity holder are interested in an increase of the equity value of a company	Debt capital provider are not very interested in an increased value of the company. They only want they capital with interests back

Equity financing is economically the most expensive form of financing since dividends are not tax-deductible (as can be seen in the table).

Types of equity

Preferred shares

Preferred shares are issued by stock corporations. These shares have some privileges as opposed to common stocks. Preferred shares have a priority right to the profit of the company (dividends). They receive a limited dividend payout before the common stockholder receives any dividend. Furthermore, preferred shares can be provided with a makeup. If the company is not making any profit in a given year the preferred share will receive the missed payouts in later years when there is profit to distribute (to the cost of the common shareholder since there might not be much profit left for them in a given year). These advantages of the preferred shares come with the cost that they do not have a right of co-determination as the common shares have.

In case of insolvency the preferred shares take a special status as opposed to the common shares. They get their invested money back before the common shareholder does (if there is still money left after paying the debtholders first).

Shareholder loan

The shareholder loan (sometimes called fixed-return instrument) is provided by the shareholders of the company. It is similar to a loan provided by a bank; however, this loan is provided by the shareholder, so the private equity fund in case of a buyout. Depending on the exact structure and form, the loan is recorded under liabilities or equity in the balance sheet (mostly as equity). The interest payments are to a certain extent tax-deductible. Tax-deductibility depends largely on the exact structure of the loan and on the tax authorities. The loan can be structured in the way that the interest payments are cumulated and paid at maturity. This is called bullet repayment as all interest and the repayments are paid together at the end as a "bullet." Although the shareholder loan might be seen as equity, it does not increase in value. If the common equity increases in value, it will only earn the interest. In case of insolvency, the shareholder loan is subordinated to any other loans. This is one of the reasons why the shareholder loan is seen by banks and other capital providers as equity and therefore generally treated as equity in the balance sheet.

<u>Equity provided by the Management (Sweet equity)</u>

As already mentioned it is extremely important for the private equity fund that the management is highly motivated to increase the profitability and the value of the company. However, between the private equity fund and the management exists the "principal–agent problem." This problem or theory occurs when there is an information asymmetry between the principal (in this case the private equity fund) and the agent (in this case the management of the company). Since the principal does not want to manage the day-to-day business of the company, he hires the agent to do this. By managing the business, the agent has an information advantage over the principal. According to the "principal–agent theory," the management will first of all only care about its own interest, which might be to get the highest possible salary with the lowest number of work hours. In addition, the management might be interested in spending the company's money on nice things (for the management) such as a corporate plane or helicopter. Besides, since the management has an information advantage, it can find excuses for chartering the plane, or for the company's poor financial performance (when actually the management is just not putting in the effort).

The principal–agent problem can be tackled by aligning the interests of the principal and the agent. The main interest of the private equity fund is to increase the equity value of the company. If the management receives a meaningful share of the equity, the interests are mainly aligned. Therefore, the private equity fund wants the management to invest their own money in the company. The management needs to have some "skin in the game." The amount of money invested depends on the personal wealth of the management. It does not matter if it is not a lot of money since the management generally only has a small fortune compared to the money necessary to acquire the equity of the company. What is important is that the management would not like to lose the money it is investing (which would be the case if the company is performing bad). However, it should not be existence-threatening as this would support irrational decision-making by the management. In general, the amount invested is at least equal to the annual gross income of the management.

However, this amount is often not high enough for the management to acquire a meaningful share in the company so that it is completely motivated to increase the value. Hence, the management receives the equity for favorable conditions; in other words, it receives equity shares much cheaper. This equity is called sweet equity. The ratio of what the private equity fund pays to what the management pays for the equity is called envy ratio. The formula for calculating the envy ratio is as follows:

$$\frac{\frac{Investment\ of\ the\ PE\ fund}{Stake\ of\ the\ PE\ fund\ in\ \%}}{\frac{Investment\ of\ the\ management}{Stake\ of\ the\ management\ in\ \%}}$$

In our example calculation, it is assumed that the enterprise value of a company which is available for sale is USD 500 million. The acquisition price is financed with USD 300 million in debt and the remaining USD 200 million with equity. The private equity fund contributes USD 190 million as shareholder loan which is seen as equity. Furthermore, it provides USD 8 million in common stocks. The management provides USD 2 million in common stocks. This results in an equity stake for the private equity fund of 80% (USD 8 million out of USD 10 million in common stocks) and for the management 20% equity stake (USD 2 million out of USD 10 million in common stocks).

The envy ratio amounts to: $\dfrac{\left(\dfrac{198}{80\,\%}\right)}{\left(\dfrac{2}{20\,\%}\right)} = 24.75$

The higher the envy ratio is, the more the private equity fund has paid for its stake in the company compared to the management. The ratio shows how much more the fund needs to pay for the same equity stake compared to the management. In the example, the management pays USD 0.1 million for 1% of the equity (1% * USD 2 million / 20% = USD 0.1 million). The private equity fund pays for 1% equity: 0.1 * 24.75 = USD 2.475 million (1% * 198 million / 80% = 2.475).

Whether the envy ratio should be calculated on the acquisition date or the exit date depends on the private equity fund. However, it should be noted that the result of the envy ratio is often different between the acquisition date and exit date. This is due to the changing common equity value compared to the shareholder loan (assuming the equity value increases over time).

Types of debt

<u>Senior debt</u>

Senior debt is probably used in every private equity transaction. Senior debt is paid back first in case of insolvency and therefore seen as a relatively secure form of debt. Only if there is still liquidity left after the senior debt is paid back, other capital provider will be served. Generally, there are three different forms of senior debt: senior term notes, bridge loans, and revolving credit facilities.

The senior term notes regularly provide the largest part of the acquisition debt. The word "term" means that the loan is exclusively used for the acquisition financing and not for investments or alike. Stakes in the company are often used as a collateral; however, if assets are not already used as collateral for other loans, they can also be used for the senor term notes. The amount of the notes particularly depends on the expected cash flows of the company. After all, the expected cash flows are needed to pay back the notes. The senior term notes in most leveraged buyouts are split into three tranches (A, B, and C tranches). Term Loan A is provided for around five to seven years. Term Loan B has a slightly longer duration, around seven to eight years. Furthermore, Loan B is often paid back as a bullet payment (interest and repayments are cumulated and paid at maturity). Owing to the longer duration and the bullet payment, Loan B has a higher interest rate than Loan A (currently around 50 basis points, or 0.5%). Loan C has a duration of around eight to nine years and is structured as a bullet payment. The interest rate is around 100 basis points (1%) higher than Loan A. Often, all the collateral is used for securing Loan A, which is why this tranche is often called secured senior debt. The B and C tranches are thus called unsecured senior debt. In large transactions, it is possible to use even more tranches (D, E, F…). This allows for a good risk–return allocation.

Bridge loans

Bridge loans are used to bridge financing gaps. If, for example, the plan is to issue public bonds, this can often take a few months to complete. In that case, it makes sense to get a bridge loan from a bank.

Revolving credit facility ("Revolver")

The revolving credit facility is a credit line which can be used if the available cash flows are not high enough to pay the mandatory interest and repayments of certain loans. However, the credit facility can also be used for other expenses. Often the credit facility is used for working capital expenses. The facility does not necessarily need to be used and also the amount used can vary (a maximal amount is agreed "the credit line"). Hence, this is a very flexible credit instrument and bears comparison with a credit card. In case the facility is not used at all by the company, it generally needs to pay a commitment fee (e.g. 0.5% of the credit line). If the facility is used, the company has to pay interest on the amount used. In addition, the repayment of the facility can be made considerably flexible. A revolving credit facility is important for leveraged buyouts since the exact future cash flows needed for the senior debt repayment cannot be planned 100% accurately. The revolving credit facility provides some flexibility.

Second-lien loan

Second-lien loans can be placed between senior debt and mezzanine capital. This kind of loans evolved in connection to very large leveraged buyouts and are regularly quite margin strong for the banks (400–700 basis points). The duration of second-lien loans is often longer than the duration of senior loans. As with the senior loans, the second-lien loans can be split in different trances. They are subordinated to the senior debt which means that they have a higher interest rate. The interest and repayments are regularly structured as bullet payment (paid cumulatively at maturity). Second-lien loans can make sense if more expensive loans can be replaced by the second-lien loans.

Seller loan

As the name suspects, the seller loan is a loan provided by the seller. Thus, a part of the purchase price is deferred and paid at the agreed maturity. A seller loan increases the trust of the acquirer since the seller is for the time being waving a part of the purchase price. The loan is generally subordinated to bank loans, and the seller does not get any collateral for the loan. Under such conditions, the seller shows obviously that he is believing in the future of the company to be able to repay the loans (at least). For the acquirer, the obvious advantage is that he does not have to pay 100% of the purchase price at the time of the acquisition. As with the second-line loan, both the interest and the repayments are cumulated and paid at maturity.

The seller loan can be structured in such a way that the interest rate is higher than the "market" interest rate for such loans. This would result in a present value which is higher than the market present value of the loan. The difference could be subtracted from the part of the purchase price the acquirer has to pay immediately. This would further reduce the amount the acquirer has to pay immediately. The lower starting acquisition price is then obviously equalized with the higher interest rates for the seller loan. Therefore, a part of the purchase price is paid via higher interest rates. This can also be structured in the opposite direction. This would mean that the interest rate is lower than the "market" interest rates, and that the acquisition price is therefore increased by the difference. The agreed interest rates for a seller loan can therefore be quite different depending on what is agreed on.

Profit-participating loan

A profit-participating loan does not have a fixed return or interest. Rather, the return depends on certain success factors of the company. These success factors need to be agreed on. An example is that the loan holder receives a certain percentage of the annual EBITDA or the annual net income of the company. Since the EBITDA and the net income changes each year, the return is variable. In the balance sheet, the profit-participating loan is treated as debt since the loan is not participating in any losses of the company. This means that if the company makes losses, the face value of the loan does not decrease.

If the profit-participating loan includes an equity option (also called equity kicker), the loan can be seen as mezzanine capital.

Subordinated debt or junior debt

Subordinated debt (often also called junior debt) is subordinated to the other forms of debt and therefore it has a higher interest rate. Typically, subordinated debt is repaid as a pullet payment (interest and repayments). Additionally, this debt can be structured with an equity kicker which would reduce the interest rate. The equity kicker gives the creditor the right (not the obligation) to exchange part or all of the debt in equity. This would allow the creditor to participate in the success of the company. However, this obviously leads to a dilution of the old shareholder structure. Still this form of mezzanine can make sense for a company when it cannot get any senior debt anymore and still needs capital but does not want to (or can) raise equity.

Mezzanine capital

A standard definition of the term "mezzanine capital" is not found in the business sciences. "Mezzanine" is originally Italian and describes in architecture the mezzanine between two main floors. Mezzanine is simplified an intermediate between equity and debt. Thus, it has characteristics of equity and of debt. Owing to the principle of freedom of contract, the contract parties have many possibilities to structure the mezzanine capital. Hence, it is not possible to generalize the exact forms of mezzanine capital. However, some main attributes of mezzanine capital should be pointed out:

- It is subordinated in relation to other creditors in case of an insolvency and prior the "real" equity holder
- In comparison to classic debt the mezzanine capital is more expensive (e.g. through higher interest payments). Furthermore, it includes a performance-related remuneration (e.g. the return depends on the success of the company)
- The expenses for the mezzanine capital are generally tax-deductible for the debtor (e.g. the target company). Exceptions are generally atypical silent partnerships
- The mezzanine capital is generally provided only for a limited amount of time (often between five and ten years)
- They do not have a dilution of the shareholder structure (apart from mezzanine with equity kicker components)
- Generally, they do not use any collateral which increases the ability of the debtor to receive a higher amount of regular debt

In the following, typical mezzanine structures are explained briefly.

Convertible bonds

Convertible bonds are bonds that are publicly traded on stock exchanges (which is why they are not so often used in private equity-led transactions). The market has many different forms of convertible bonds with different names.

A convertible bond guarantees the right to exchange a bond for a stock (equity) in a defined exchange ratio. It is thereby like the equity kicker in the subordinated debt. The debt claim is destroyed with the conversion. This is different from the option bond, where the debt claim stays after the conversion. The central part of the convertible bond is obviously the conversion ratio (i.e. how much equity I get for a given bond) with which the bond can be converted into equity.

Participation certificate

The participation certificate securitizes a participation right. Through the securitization a right becomes tradeable.[24] Participation certificates are thus claims toward the issuer (the company that issues the participation certificates) for a share in the profit of the company. In other words, if the company is being liquidized the certificate owner is entitled to some of the proceeds. Hence, the certificate owner is not an owner of the company. Participation certificates are legally not regulated a lot,

---

[24] Securitization became famous (in a negative way) during the financial crisis of 2008. Loans were securitized and then re-securitized with other securitizations, often more than just once. The resulting complexity of this securitization is considered one of the reasons for the financial crisis.

which offers the parties many possibilities as to how to structure the certificate. Therefore, the certification terms should at least include some agreements about the maturity, seniority, cancellation conditions, and repayment. Participation certificates provide any decision-making rights; they only hold information rights. This means the holder cannot decide on the strategy of the company; however, he is allowed to receive information about how the company is doing.

The participation certificate can be structured so that the holder also participates in the losses of the company. The certificate can be placed as equity in the balance sheet of the issuer. However, according to the IFRS (International Financial Reporting Standard), this is only allowed when the certificate has no fixed interest payments and the certificate-holder cannot demand repayment of the certificate. The many different forms of the participation certificate can make the use of it interesting for a private equity fund.

Further purchase price financing forms

Earn-out

Instead of agreeing right from the beginning on a fixed purchase price, the price can also be made flexible, depending on the future development of the company. This means that it is agreed on certain factors that measure the success of the company in the future. Depending on the success, the acquirer has to pay a higher or lower amount in the future (e.g. after three years). This agreement is called an earn-out and is often used when it is hard to value the company (e.g. a medical technology company that is launching a new major product soon) and the parties thus have problems agreeing on a purchase price. Branches like the pharma industry are generally not easy to valuate, especially smaller companies that are dependent on the success of the next medicine.

In a classical earn-out, a seller will receive money during the acquisition as well as after some years (e.g. three years) if certain conditions are fulfilled. Understandably, it is not that easy to structure such an earn-out. After all, the earn-out needs to be structured in such a way that the acquirer cannot influence the results so that he does not have to pay any money after three years, for example. The timeframe in which the success is measured should not be too short in order to prevent manipulations possible by the acquirer. In order to motivate the acquirer to work hard on the success, the contract should be structured in such a way that the acquirer will get a part of the proceeds above the success hurdle. The EBITDA could be, for example, a success measure. It could be agreed that the EBITDA needs to result in USD 50 million or more in order for the seller to receive money from the earn-out. The amount the seller receives should only be a portion (e.g. 50%) of the amount above USD 50 million, with the rest staying with the acquirer.

The earn-out has the obvious advantage that he is likely not paying a price which is too high for the company. The seller, on the other hand, creates a lot of trust with the earn-out since he believes that the company will perform well. It is likely that the price he receives with the earn-out is higher than if he would agree on a fixed price paid at acquisition.

Covenants

The many different possibilities of structuring the acquisition financing result in comprehensive loan and syndication contracts. These contracts include detailed regulations about the restrictions and duties of the debtor. It also includes regulations about when the debt provider needs to be informed about certain events. These regulations are called covenants (sometimes also called undertakings). These covenants are a kind of a control and warning system that informs the creditors if the company is not doing well. This enables creditors to react in a timely manner.

Financial covenants are precisely defined figures, which, depending on the conditions, cannot be exceeded or fallen short of. The figures are agreed on before the credit contract is signed. The figures need to be reported by the company on a quarterly or yearly basis. Independent auditors (like Deloitte, EY, KPMG, and PwC) often audit these figures and report them in a compliance certificate.

If the covenants are not fulfilled (or breached) it is generally possible for the creditor to demand the loan back immediately (cancel the loan contract). However, this is in practice often not done if the non-fulfilment happens for the first time. Nevertheless, the possibility to demand the loan back puts the creditors in a comfortable position to renegotiate the credit conditions. The creditors could demand that the interest rate on the loan be increased. This is often already agreed on in the loan contract in the first place. The increase in the interest rate (and thereby margin) in case of a covenant breach is called default margin. Furthermore, the creditors can demand that the covenants be fulfilled. This can be done with an equity injection by the shareholder or by providing more collateral for the loans. The creditors can demand a restructuring of the company if it is not possible for the management to fulfil the covenants. This restructuring is often done by specialized consultants. Further options are the replacement of the management of the company. In any case, a breach of covenants can lead to a power shift from the equity holder to the debt holder.

There are, in addition to the financial covenants, certain behavioral covenants (also called general undertakings) that need to be fulfilled. These include, for example, the behavior of the debtor in case of an acquisition, capital increase, restructuring, dividends, and guaranties against third parties.

The following table shows some sample financial covenants which can be included in loan contracts:

Financial covenant	Formula and definition of the elements	Comment
Total leverage (also called leverage cover)	$$\frac{\text{Net debt}}{\text{EBITDA}}$$ Net debt: All interest bearing liabilities (e.g. all Term Notes etc.) minus cash and cash equivalents	Maximal condition which means that the agreed multiple can't be exceeded in order to not breach the covenant, e.g. if agreed multiple is 4x than net debt need to be low or EBITDA high enough to not reach 4x
Senior leverage ratio	$$\frac{\text{Net Senior debt}}{\text{EBITDA}}$$ Net senior debt: All remaining senior debt minus cash and cash equivalents	Maximal condition, as above however only with senior debt
Cash cover	$$\frac{\text{Operating cashflow}}{\text{Debt service}}$$ Debt service: Cash interest and repayments	Minimal condition, the agreed multiple needs to be met and can't be fallen short of; the yearly operative cashflows need to be high enough to meet all interest- and repayments. The cash cover is regularly agreed to be at least 1:1

Interest cover	$\dfrac{EBITDA}{\text{Net interest expenses}}$ Net interest expenses: All interest expenses (e.g. for the senior debt) subtracted by any interest income	Minimal condition; This covenant provides a multiple of how much the operative performance (measured in EBITDA) can pay the net interest expenses
Debt/Equity ratio	$\dfrac{\text{Debt}}{\text{Equity}}$	Maximal condition

Structuring of the acquisition

As already mentioned, private equity funds create acquisition entities to acquire the target company. In the annual report of the Germany-based private equity firm Deutsche Beteiligungs AG from 2016, it is mentioned that they are invested in 46 entities most of which are acquisition entities.

The following graphic shows the planned shareholding structure of the acquisition of Hugo Boss AG (German apparel retailer) by Permira. The graph is from the public takeover offering which Permira had made in 2007 to the Hugo Boss shareholder.

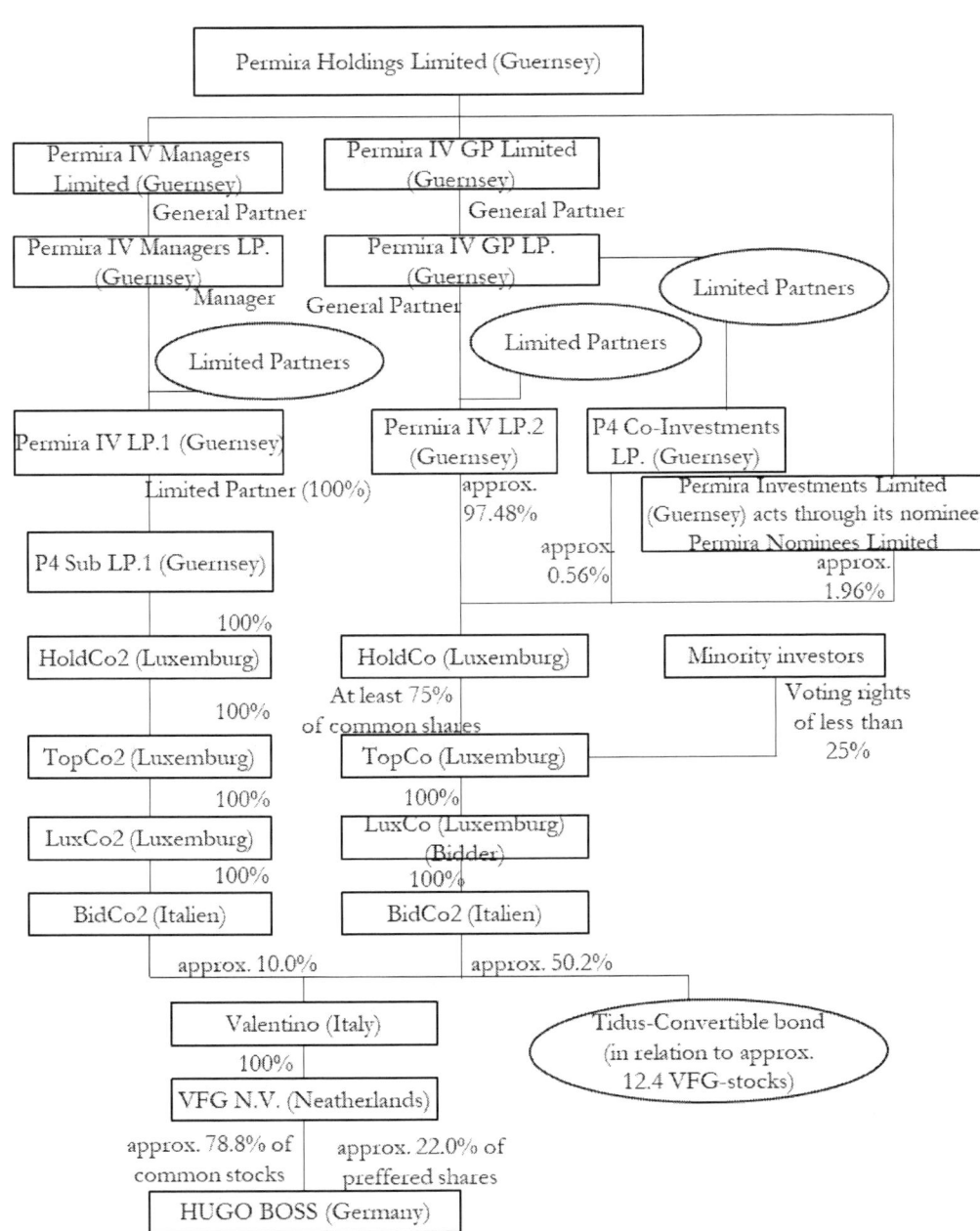

Permira acquired the Italy-based Valentino Group first since they were the largest shareholder of Hugo Boss. As can be seen, the acquisition structures can be quite complex. This is due to organizational, legal, and tax reasons.

The tax reasons are explained in the following:

Tax expenses are different from capital expenditures since tax expenses cannot be shaped. They are strictly and in a timely manner collected by the tax authorities. Therefore, private equity funds need to plan the tax expenses very precisely, especially when a lot of debt is used for the acquisition. Low tax expenses have a higher value for private equity transactions in comparison to other M&A deals (e.g. by strategic acquirer). The optimal structuring of the company acquisition has the following aims:

- No or very low tax expenses at exit
- Tax-deductibility of the debt interest
- Avoiding withholding tax[25] for dividends and interest at the country of occurrence
- Excess of the debt financing banks to the cash flows without tax disadvantages
- Appropriate breakthrough rights for the private equity fund

The following graph shows a simplified transaction model which is often used by Anglo–Saxon private equity funds:

---

[25] Withholding tax can be claimed by the country where the income is created. For example, when a company form Luxemburg is investing in a Germany-based company. If the German company pays dividends, the German government could make the Luxemburg company pay taxes on the dividend.

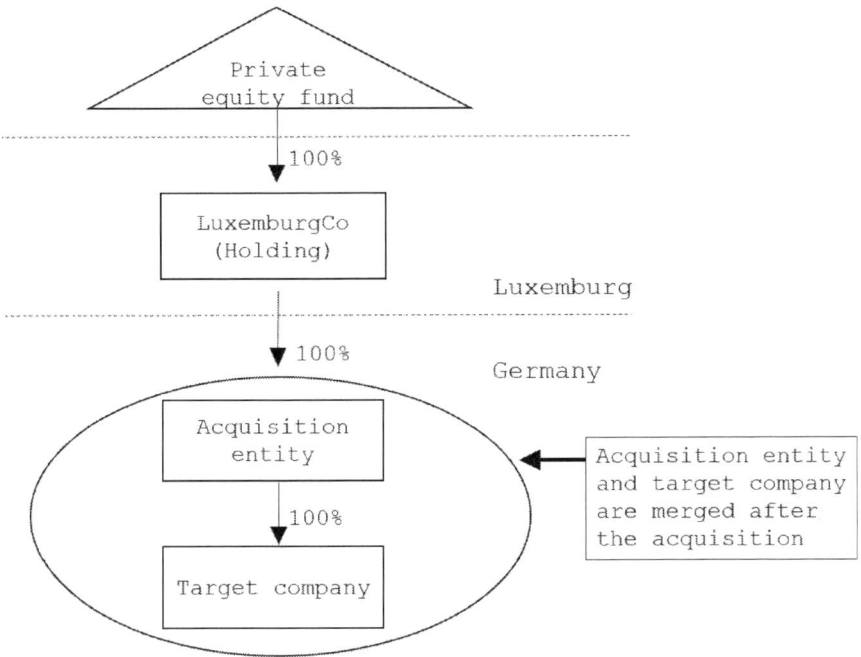

The purpose of the acquisition entity in Luxemburg (other tax optimized countries are possible too) is to prevent that the exit (sale) proceeds of the private equity fund are taxed. The LuxemburgCo is as a corporation in Luxemburg, a taxable entity. According to current Luxemburg tax law, exit proceeds and dividends are tax free if the LuxemburgCo holds at least 10% of the shares of the subsidiary (here acquisition entity). Alternatively, it can hold a share of at least EUR 1.2 million for a timeframe of twelve month without interruptions. Furthermore, the amount of debt used currently cannot exceed 85% of the overall capital used.

If the subsidiary (target company) of a Luxembourgish corporation is sold, the Luxembourgish corporation needs to have, according to the double taxation agreement (between Germany and Luxemburg), enough **substance** for the net proceeds to be tax free. Therefore, the domicile (§ 11 AO, German law) as well as the senior management (§ 10 AO, German law) needs to be in Luxemburg. This means that the daily decisions also need to be made in Luxemburg. Especially with respect to documentation, this is a challenge. The Luxembourgish corporation needs to prove that they have a business address, office space, along with employment relationships. In practice, especially the controlling activities should be done in Luxemburg.

Owing to finance and tax reasons, it is important that the fund brings the debt (which it raised to pay for the acquisition) to the level of the target company. This process is called **debt pushdown**. The debt and the operating profits of the target company are on one level due to the debt pushdown. Interest and repayments for the debt can then be cleared against the profits without having to pay out any dividends to the acquisition entity (which would then have to pay back the debt). Furthermore, this process allows the target company to deduct the interest payments from the taxable income. In addition, the debt provider (banks and alike) often demand that the debt is on the same level as the operating profits.

A debt pushdown can be done by merging or consolidating the acquisition entity and the target company.

Merger/Consolidation

In a merger, two or more companies are combined in one corporation with only one of the companies surviving (the acquisition entity merges with the target company with the target company being the remaining on). In a consolidation, two or more companies are combined in one new corporation. In this example, the acquisition entity and the target companies form one new company.

Another way to achieve a debt pushdown is by doing a debt-financed dividend payment. After the acquisition, the acquisition entity will receive a dividend payment from the target company in the amount of the desired debt pushdown. However, the dividend payment is not actually paid, and the target company takes the liabilities from the acquisition loans.

SPA = Sales and purchase agreement[26]

The last important part of the M&A process is the negotiation of the SPA. Generally, this negotiation can take some time and be stressful for all parties. After all, the SPA is the main contract of a transaction. The seller wants to define clear rules regarding the acquisition price and when the money needs to be paid. Furthermore, he wants to provide as few guarantees[27] as possible.

The acquirer, on the other hand, wants a low purchase price and as many guarantees as possible.

The elements of a successful SPA negotiation are that the risks and chances of the transaction are distributed to both parties equally. As already mentioned the SPA is different depending on if it is a share or an asset deal.

---

[26] An example SPA can be found on: http://www.mbauction.com/assets/Sale-and-Purchase-Agreement-SAMPLE.pdf
[27] The acquire could for example demand from the seller that he guarantees that no crucial employee wanted or threatened to quit working for the company if it is sold.

4. Post-investment phase

After the private equity fund acquired the target company, it is all about increasing the value of the company (now a "portfolio company"). This phase is called the post-investment phase. The post-investment phase claims most of the time of the investment process. According to studies the tasks in this phase uses around 60% of the time of the private equity manager.[28] However, it also depends on the level of the individual manager of the fund. For example, the associates (around 3–6 years' work experience) spend a lot of time working with the portfolio companies (post-investment phase), whereas the senior partner (highest management level of a private equity fund) is more responsible for fundraising and deal sourcing (finding the right target companies).

One action to increase the company's value is by making use of the leverage effect. A study by Achleitner et al. (2010) investigating 206 buyouts found that the value creation through an increased use of leverage makes around 32%. The remaining 68% of value creation come from operative and/or strategic initiatives.

Some private equity funds do not initiate many value-creation actions and leave it up to the management. This passive attitude is called the "hands-off" approach. Many studies (e.g. Achleitner et al. [2010]), however, suggest that an active attitude ("hands-on" approach) is more likely to create value.

---

[28] Brettel, M.; Kauffmann, C.; Kühn, C.; Sobczak, C (2008), p. 96

Private equity funds try to increase the cash flows with certain initiatives (executed by the company's management) which will lead to an increased enterprise value. The main focus is on the optimization of the working capital to increase the cash flows.

In general, the initiatives can be divided into three categories. In the category **monitoring,** the monitoring and controlling of the portfolio company takes place. Monitoring is also done in private equity funds that take a hands-off approach. In the category **mentoring,** the fund manager supports the management of the portfolio company with advice and help. The last category, **intervening,** is used only when the company does not grow as the fund planned it to do. In the following, the three categories will be explained in more detail.

100-day Plan

A 100-day plan is a plan which the private equity firm and the target management create during or right after due diligence. This plan describes actions that are planned to be done in the first 100 days after the acquisition. It includes, for example, deep analyses of required operational improvements. In a survey, advisory firm Grant Thornton LPP found that almost 90% of private equity firms use a 100-day plan.[29] The plan provides a well-thought-out and structured way of making the first initiatives. This allows the management and the private equity fund to "hit the ground running" right after the acquisition is completed.

---

[29] Grant Thornton LPP and PitchBook: "What can be done in 100 days?" October 2013

Monitoring

Since the capital of the fund remains tied to the portfolio company for some years, monitoring is crucial. The fund needs to know about the economic and financial situation of the portfolio company. This allows the fund to react in a timely manner if the company is not doing great. The risk of losing some or all the money can be reduced by this. However, the permanent monitoring of the company takes time and costs the fund money (salary of the fund managers). As already mentioned in the remuneration section, other shareholders profit from the monitoring of the fund (they do not need to monitor the company as much anymore, the free-riding principle). Therefore, often a monitoring fee is agreed to compensate the fund for its monitoring effort.

To receive all information needed for monitoring, the fund needs to include already in the participation agreement all relevant information and control rights. Hence, due diligence (before the acquisition) is also intended to review the quality of the company's information (or controlling) systems. This information lays the foundation for all upcoming decisions, which is why it needs to be precise and up to date. If the information systems are not good, the private equity fund can either demand the company to make investments in this area (which would be a value creation initiative), or choose not to acquire the company at all.

Usually, the private equity fund demands monthly, or at least quarterly, reports from the company. These reports need to provide updated income statements, balance sheets, and cash flow statements. Besides, detailed investment and business plans are provided if appropriate. What is more, reports about the current state of product developments, detailed sale figures, order backlog as well as marketing successes or alike could be asked for.

The development of the business will be compared to the business plan the private equity fund made during the due diligence process. If the company is not performing as good as the private equity fund planned it to do (during due diligence), the fund can take appropriate actions.

To be closer to the decisions of the company, a private equity fund manager can take a seat in the supervisory board of the company. This is very often done in the German-speaking countries. However, due to legal reasons (liability risks), this is not so common in Anglo-Saxon countries such as the U.S.

Another way of achieving a valuable information flow is by agreeing on a catalogue of business decisions that need approval. If the company wants to execute a decision which will have a meaningful effect, it will have to get the approval from the private equity fund first. Generally, this also includes larger investments. A seat on the supervisory board and the catalogue of approval-requiring decisions are effective ways of influencing the strategic decisions.

Mentoring

The act of monitoring does not actively initiate value-creation activities. Mentoring, however, regularly leads to value-creation initiatives. In particular, monitoring involves providing management advice and helping with the fund's network. The intensity of mentoring always depends on the fund (e.g. hands-on or hands-off) and the specifics of the company (e.g. if it is currently implementing a main strategic change or has some trouble). Mentoring will be most fruitful when the management of the portfolio company realizes the value of mentoring and appreciates the advice. Already before the acquisition, the private equity fund will signalize the advantage of mentoring and a regular exchange of ideas. The support by the fund spreads often over all the business fields of a company. Fund managers have decades of experience in the field of the portfolio company. This allows the fund to advise the company not only in their core fields like the structuring of the liability site (especially helping the company during negotiations with banks) and the advice during acquisitions. It allows them to help in fields like human resource, strategy, product development, as well as marketing and sales.

Owing to the external perspective on the portfolio company, it is sometimes more obvious for the funds professionals to see certain improvement opportunities. They can also draw on their experience from past portfolio companies where they might have had a comparable situation. What is more, they have an extensive network of experts whom they can ask for advice if needed. These experts can often provide the fund with the right manager who can help the company. This saves the fund management time as well as money in investments in the wrong senior management. The following graph shows possible initiatives which the portfolio manager can do with the help of the fund manager.

	Value creation	Private Equity Fund experience

Revenue	• Use and creation of the organic- / market growth
	  - New strategy (new products and/or Geographic's)
	  - Capex (Capital expenditures)
	• Increase of scale
	  - Lead consolidation of the industry
	  - Acquisition of add-on targets (buy and build strategy)
		• Support of the management in the current strategy or development of a new one
		  - Use of experience from other portfolio companies
		  - Hiring third party advisors (e.g. strategy consulting firms)
		• Increase of scale
		  - Improving excess to the capital market through network of the private equity fund (As an example: the financing cost of the Hugo Boss AG decreased significantly after the company was acquired by the private equity firm Permira)
		  - Advise doing acquisitions

x		

EBITDA-margin	• Improving the margin
	  - Optimisation of the product mix
	  - Improving product pricing
	  - Use of scale effects
	  - Reducing the fixed costs
	• Restructuring
	  - Reducing costs / Operative improvements
	  - Generate synergies
		• Improving the margin
		  - Use of experience from other portfolio companies
		  - Hiring third party advisors (e.g. strategy consulting firms)
		• Restructuring
		  - Best practice as well as knowledge transfer from the private equity fund to the portfolio company
		  - Possible synergies with other portfolio companies

x		

Exit multiple	• Improving the equity story (improved communication and explanation of the company towards the capital market)
	  - Repositioning the company
	  - Reach of critical mass
	  - Assessing other exit channels
	• Creation of „multiple arbitrage" (Increasing the exit multiple compared to the entry multiple)
		• Improving the equity story
		  - Increase of companies prominence (e.g. through M&A advisor)
		  - Incentivise management to increase alignment of interests
		• Creation of „multiple arbitrage"
		  - Identification and acquisition of undervalued assets
		  - Use of the cycle in order to buy low and sell high

=		
	Exit Enterprise Value	

A study done by the Boston Consulting Group (BCG) in 2012 found that a commonly used initiative to create value is through the acquisition of further companies, also called buy-and-build strategy[30]. The resulting synergies through buy-and-build can facilitate excellent value creation. This initiative is followed by entering new countries. The study asked private equity manager what initiatives they use to create value. Value creations can also result through a great exit. This is especially the case when the market is in a great condition and is paying higher multiples than the fund paid for the acquisition (e.g. EBITDA multiple at exit of 10 instead of 9). If the company is sold for a higher multiple than it was bought for, it is called "multiple riding."

---

[30] In a buy-and-build strategy, a private equity fund acquires one company and then builds on that through add-on acquisitions.

5. Exit – The sale of the portfolio company

The last step of a leveraged buyout is the sale of the portfolio company (exit). In general, the private equity fund hires an investment bank (M&A department) to organize the sale. The private equity fund has a clear advantage over a lot of other shareholders who want to sell their companies. The fund has already extensive experience in selling a company.

There are different exit channels that can be used to sell the company. These channels and their advantages and disadvantages will be explained in the following.

Sale to a strategic acquirer (also called trade sale)

The sale to a strategic acquirer is one of the most commonly used exit channels. A strategic buyer is a company that hopes to gain synergies or other strategic goals with the acquisition. These buyers are often active in the same industry as the portfolio company. Synergies can for example be realized when the logistics systems of both companies are merged into one large one. This can help to save costs and increase efficiency.

A further reason for the acquisition could be that the acquirer wants to enter a new market segment in which the portfolio company is already successful. Furthermore, it may want to sell its product in countries where it is not selling yet but the portfolio company is.

Owing to the synergies and a possible strategic fit, the strategic acquirer can often pay a much higher price than other acquirers (e.g. a private equity fund). Hence, private equity funds often sell their portfolio companies to strategic acquirers. The disadvantage of this channel is that it can sometimes take a bit more time and is also not as certain to be completed as, for example, a secondary buyout (sale to another private equity fund).

Initial public offering (IPO)

An exit channel that is likely to be the most expensive and time-consuming is the initial public offering (going public). The portfolio company needs to have a certain size to make the IPO worth the effort (and to be allowed to do it). Furthermore, before a company can go public it needs to meet certain regulatory requirements. Before an IPO the company regularly does a roadshow to attract investors, which is organized by investment banker (equity capital markets department). The roadshow can take some management capacity away from the day-to-day business of the company which needs to be considered. What is very important during the IPO process is that the stock market is in a healthy state. The condition of the stock market will influence the realized price significantly. Owing to the financial crisis of 2007/8, as well as the EURO crisis, this exit channel has not been used that much by private equity funds lately. However, if the market is in good conditions and provides high valuation, this channel can provide a very lucrative exit.

Secondary buyout

If the fund sells the portfolio company to another private equity fund, it is called a secondary buyout. This form of exit has increased in importance over the years as the private equity industry is growing. This channel can be executed more quickly and has more certainty to be completed than a trade sale and an IPO. This is because both parties (seller and buyer) often have a lot of experience in executing transactions. However, the acquirer needs to have a clear vision about how he wants to further create value for the company. This is because all "low hanging fruits" were already harvested by the previous private equity fund. Often a secondary buyout makes sense for the acquirer if it has experience in growing companies by further add-on acquisitions and more internationalization initiatives. Furthermore, it might be that the seller needs to sell the company because of the maturity of the fund despite value creation opportunities still left to be done.

Dual-track

If a trade sale as well as an IPO is prepared, it is called a dual-track. This exit channel is obviously quite time and money consuming. The strategic investor needs to be contacted, all IPO-related regulations need to be implemented, and a roadshow needs to be organized. However, it has some interesting advantages. If a strategic investor offers a very attractive price, the IPO can be cancelled and the transaction completed without significant risk. If no strategic investor offers an attractive price, the IPO can be pursued. Owing to the mentioned stock market turbulences of the last years, this channel has become more attractive.

Selecting the right exit channel

Finding the right exit channel depends always on the specific portfolio company as well as the current market conditions. As already mentioned, some portfolio companies are just not large enough for an IPO. The costs as well as the necessary management capacity of each channel need to be considered as well. This means that it is decided case by case which channel is the right one.

6. Leveraged buyout (LBO) valuation

As opposed to the strategic acquirer, which values a company with the discounter cash flow (DCF) and the multiple valuation, a private equity fund uses mainly the leveraged buyout (LBO) valuation. However, this does not mean that they do not use other methods like the DCF and the multiple valuation.

The purpose of LBO valuation is not to find the value of a company but to find the right financing structure of the company. The LBO model (which is what the Excel LBO valuation is called) illustrates how much debt a company's cash flow can bear while still complying with covenants. Moreover, the LBO valuation is a sensitivity analysis because different scenarios are calculated.

Note on the model:
The model outlined here is a practical introduction to LBO valuation. To increase comprehensibility, some simplifications were done since an extensive model can quickly become quite complex. At the end of this book, a reference list is given ("Literature recommendation for LBO valuations") which explains LBO valuation in more detail. It should be noted that a lot of literature is from the U.S., which uses US GAAP as the accounting standard. This will result in minor differences to the IFRS used here.

Table 6.1 shows the summarized results of the completed model. The aim of the following steps is to do all the calculations needed to get the information to fill out the *transaction summary*.

6.1 Transaction Summary (in Mio. USD)

Sources of Funds

	Amount	%	x EBITDA LTM 30.09.2015	Pricing
Revolving Credit Facility	-	- %	- x	NA
Term Loan A	350.0	21.7%	2.4x	6.0%
Term Loan B	300.0	18.6%	2.1x	6.5%
Term Loan C	300.0	18.6%	2.1x	7.0%
2nd Lien	-	- %	- x	NA
Senior Notes	-	- %	- x	NA
Total debt	**950.0**	**58.8%**	**6.6x**	
Fix Return Instrument (Equity)	605.5	37.5%	4.2x	12.5%
Ordinary Equity	10.0	0.6%	0.07x	
Private Equity Fund contrib.	8.0			
Sweet Equity	2.0			
Cash on Hand	50.0	3.1%	0.3x	
Total equity	**665.5**	**41.2%**	**4.6x**	
Total Sources	**1,615.5**	**100.0%**	**11.2x**	

Uses of Funds

	Amount	%
Purchase TargetCo. Equity	990.5	61.3%
Repay Existing Debt	500.0	31.0%
Financing Fees	95.0	5.9%
Other Fees and Expenses	30.0	1.9%
Total Uses	**1,615.5**	**100.0%**

Purchase Price

				Transaction Multiples		
Offer Price per Share	-	IRR	22.0%	Enterprise Value / EBTDA		
Fully Diluted Shares	-	Cash Return	2.7x	LTM	144.1	10.0x
Equity Purchase Price	**990.5**	Investor Return	1,321.0	2016E	163.5	8.8x
Plus: Existing Net Debt	450.0	PE Fund Return	335.0	Entry Multiple		10.0x
Enterprise Value	**1,440.5**			Exit Multiple		10.0x

Summery Credit Stats

	2015	2016E	2017E	2018E	2019E	2020E
% Debt / Total Capitalization	65.9%	62.2%	57.6%	52.1%	45.7%	39.4%
Free cash flow LTM (before interest) / Debt service		1.1x	1.3x	1.4x	1.6x	1.8x
EBITDA / Cash Interest Expense	2.4x	2.6x	3.0x	3.4x	4.0x	4.8x
EBITDA / Total Interest Expense	1.1x	1.2x	1.2x	1.3x	1.3x	1.4x
Net Debt / EBITDA	6.4x	5.5x	4.7x	3.9x	3.1x	2.4x
Total Debt / EBITDA	6.4x	5.5x	4.7x	3.9x	3.1x	2.5x

The following steps are necessary to create an LBO model:

Step 1: Creation of a pre-LBO-model

- 1.1 Creation of an income statement until EBIT for the past and future years
- 1.2 Creation of an opening balance sheet as well as projection of the balance sheet positions
- 1.3 Creation of the cash flow statement

Step 2: Creation of the transaction structure

Step 3: Creation of debt schedule and link with balance sheet, income statement and cash flow statement

Step 4: Performing the LBO-analysis and return calculation

Step 1: Creation of a pre-LBO model

1.1 Creation of an income statement until EBIT for the past and future years

Since the interest expenditures (and therefore also the tax expenditures) will change due to the leveraged buyout financial structure, the income statement is for now only done to the position EBIT. In later steps, the interest expenditure (and tax expenditures) will then be calculated in accordance to the used financial structure.

Generally, the LBO model matches the investment horizon of the private equity fund. If the fund expects to sell the company after five years, the model will be calculated until five years into the future (in the later following sensitivity analysis the timeframe can vary). Therefore, assumptions about the future balance sheet, and income and cash flow statements need to be done. To have the most precise assumptions and expectations, the private equity fund gets information from the company (e.g. information memorandum) while also using the knowledge from due diligence.

Different scenarios are created. The "management case" uses data provided by the management of the target company and has generally a rather positive view on the future of the company. Apart from that will the private equity fund create its own case "sponsor case" (private equity funds are also called sponsor, or financial sponsor). The sponsor case will especially use projections made during the due diligence process. Banks and other institutions who provide the debt for the leveraged buyout will be provided with the sponsor case. These institutions want to see the valuation to determine the terms and covenants of the loans. Nevertheless, banks and other institutions will not only rely on the sponsor case but will do their own valuations. The "base case" will provide a more conservative view on the future of the company and the market and will have the lowest growth in the projections.

1.2 Creation of an opening balance sheet as well as the projection of balance sheet positions

The numbers for the opening balance sheet are from the due diligence report. Further balance sheet positions need to be added to include the financial structure of the leveraged buyout. Revolving credit facilities or second-lien loans need to be included if, for example, they are used as a source of financing. As Table *6.6. on page 110* shows, the positions of revolving credit facility, fixed-return instrument, term loans A, B, and C were included in this model.

1.3 Creation of a cash flow statement

As in the DCF valuation, cash flow is the main part of the LBO valuation. The cash flow statement consists of the following parts: cash flow from operating activities (operating cash flow), cash flow from investing activities, cash flow from financing activities.

<u>Cash flow from operating activities</u>

To calculate the cash flow from operating activities, the respective income statement positions such depreciation and amortization (D&A) need to be used.

The first position to start with is the position **net income** from the income statement. The net income will be too high initially since the debt interest expenditures are not included yet. However, later they will be included and will reduce the net income. **Depreciations & amortizations** will be added to the net income as these expenditures are no real cash flows (non-cash expenses). Furthermore, emerge, due to the leveraged buyout character interest expenses which need to be included in the income statement, however, they do not reduce the cash available (non-cash expenses). This is because of the already mentioned bullet payment of some instruments. The interest is only paid cumulatively at the maturity of, e.g. the fixed-return instrument. These interest expenses need to be added positively to the operating cash flow (so they are treated as the D&A). In this model, only the interest for the fixed-return instrument is paid cumulatively at maturity. The interest for the term loans is paid each year as it occurs. Repayments for the loans will be made together at the end of the investment period (at exit). The change in the **net working capital**, which can be calculated by looking in the balance sheet, needs to be considered in the cash flow calculation too, as with all other balance sheet positions which are no real cash flows (non-cash).

The sum of net income, non-cash expenses (minus non-cash income), change in net working capital and **other positions (if non-cash)** result in the operating cash flow.

The following table, *Cash flow from Operating Activities*, shows the explained calculations exemplary. The net income is, as mention, currently too high, since the debt interest and the fixed-return instrument interest are not yet considered. As soon as the capital structure is incorporated in the model, the interest for the fixed-return instrument needs to be added to the operating cash flow (currently it is stated as 0). Therefore, the interest needs to be linked from the income statement into the cash flow calculation.

6.2 Cash flow from Operating Activities (in Mio. USD)

	Year 1 2016	Year 2 2017	Year 3 2018	Year 4 2019	Year 5 2020
Operating Activities					
Net income	102.0	113.2	125.4	138.1	151.7
Plus: Depreciation & Amortization	17.9	19.0	20.1	21.2	22.5
Plus: Non Cash Interest of Fix return instrument	0.0	0.0	0.0	0.0	0.0
Change in Working Capital items					
(Inc.) / Dec. in Accounts Receivable	(8.0)	(8.0)	(7.9)	(7.9)	(7.8)
(Inc.) / Dec. in Inventories	(11.0)	(10.9)	(10.8)	(10.7)	(10.6)
(Inc.) / Dec. in Other Current Assets	(0.5)	(0.3)	(0.3)	(0.2)	(0.2)
Inc. / (Dec.) in Accounts Payable	7.0	6.9	6.9	6.9	6.8
Inc. / (Dec.) in Other Current Liabilities	2.0	1.8	1.7	1.6	1.5
(Inc.) / Dec. in Net Working Capital	(10.5)	(10.4)	(10.4)	(10.3)	(10.2)
Cash flow from Operating Activities	**109.4**	**121.8**	**135.1**	**149.0**	**163.9**

Cash flow from investing activities

The largest position in the cash flow from investing activities are the capital expenditures (in short capex) which are the investments in fixed assets. Assumptions of the future capex can be taken from the due diligence report as well as the information memorandum (in this model 2% of sales were taken as assumption). The future values of the fixed assets need to include the projected capex, and therefore the yearly capex will be added to the fixed assets. What is more, the projected D&A needs to be subtracted from the fixed assets since they represent the value depreciation of the fixed assets. The sum of the cash flow from operating activities and from investing activities are available for the repayment of the debt and are often called "free cash flow."

Cash flow from financing activities

The cash flow from financing activities will not yet be calculated as it includes the repayments of the debt. In step 3 the debt schedule will be created and linked into the cash flow from financing activities. Table *6.3 on page 107* shows the structure of the financing activities cash flow. The position *Excess Cash for the Period* results from the three cash flow categories (for calculation, see Table *6.10 on page 120).*

The *Beginning Cash Balance* is from the cash and cash equivalent position from the balance sheet of the previous year (as can be seen in Table *6.3*, the ending cash balance of 2016 is the beginning cash balance in 2017). The *Excess Cash for the Period* 2016 results from the operating cash flow of USD 109.4 million minus the investment activities of USD 17.9 million. The *Ending Cash Balanced* is linked in the position cash and cash equivalents of the respective years.

6.3 Cash flow from Financing Activities (in Mio. USD)

	Year 1 2016	Year 2 2017	Year 3 2018	Year 4 2019	Year 5 2020
Financing Activities					
Equity Issuance / (Repurchase)	0.0	0.0	0.0	0.0	0.0
Dividends					
Existing Term Loan	\multicolumn{5}{c}{Is linked with the to be created debt schedule}				
Term Loan C					
Term Loan B					
Term Loan A	0.0	0.0	0.0	0.0	0.0
Revolving Credit Facility	0.0	0.0	0.0	0.0	0.0
Cash flow from Financing Activites	0.0	0.0	0.0	0.0	0.0
Excess Cash for the Period	91.5	102.8	115.0	127.8	141.5
Beginning Cash Balance	0.0	91.5	194.3	309.3	437.1
Ending Cash Balance	91.5	194.3	309.3	437.1	578.5

Is the balance sheet balanced?

When all so far mentioned steps were done right the balance sheet is balanced (sum of the total assets have the same amount as the sum of the total liabilities and the shareholders equity). If this is the case, the model is working properly and the transaction structure can be added to the model. If it is not the case, a mistake creeps in and the steps need to be redone. A common mistake is that the capex or balance sheet positions are not included in the cash flow calculation.

Step 2: Creation of the transaction structure

Assumption of an acquisition price

To determine the financial structure, a purchase price need to be assumed. If, for example, a company has an LTM (last 12 months) EBITDA of USD 144.4 million and comparable companies were sold for an EBITDA multiple of 10.0[31] on average,

---

[31] EBITDA multiple is calculated by: Enterprise value / EBITDA

the enterprise value of the company is USD 1,440.5 million (144.4 x 10.0). The equity value is calculated as shown in the following table:

6.4 Equity Value (in Mio. USD)	
Entry EBITDA Multiple	10.0x
LTM 09/30/2015	144.4
Enterprise Value	**1,440.5**
- Total Debt	(500.0)
- Preferred Securities	0.0
- Noncontrolling Interest	0.0
+ Cash and Cash Equivalent	50.0
Equity Value	**990.5**

<u>Separation of the financial structure in sources and uses of funds</u> *(Table 6.5 on page 109)*

An overview of the sources and uses of funds will be created. The sources of funds refer to where the money comes from for the acquisition. These sources include Term Loan A, Fixed-Return Instrument, and Ordinary Equity. Out of the USD 10 million in Ordinary Equity, the management (which will manage the company after the transaction) will contribute USD 2 million. It will therefore receive 20% of the company's shares (sweet equity). With that, the management directly participates in the company's profit or loss, and is highly motivated to manage the company as good as possible. The interest of the management and that of the private equity fund are therefore aligned.

For the debt part of the sources, the private equity fund can assume its preferred amount for now. In a later analysis, it will be seen if the preferred amount of debt can be carried by the company's cash flow (measured with the covenants). In this model, the debt amount will be set at around 60% of the transaction volume for now.

The uses of the funds show for what the funds were used, e.g. for the company's equity, for the repayment of the old debt or for the transaction costs (e.g. for advisory fees from M&A advisors).

The sources and the uses need to match. As can be seen in Table *6.5,* the sources and uses amount to USD 1,615.5 million and are therefore USD 175.0 million higher than the previously calculated enterprise value of USD 1,440.5 million. This is because the cash on hand (USD 50.0 million) is used for the financing as well as the transaction fees (Financing Fees + Other Fees and Expenses = USD 125 million) that need to be paid.

6.5 Sources and Uses of Funds (in Mio. USD)			
Sources of Funds		Uses of Funds	
	Amount		Amount
Debt		Purchase Equity	990.5
Term Loan A	350.0	Repay Existing Debt	500.0
Term Loan B	300.0	Financing Fees	95.0
Term Loan C	300.0	Other Fees and Expenses	30.0
Equity			
Fixed Return Instrument (Equity)	605.5		
Ordinary Equity	10.0		
Cash on Hand	50.0		
Total Source	**1,615.5**	**Total Uses**	**1,615.5**

The sources need to be linked in the opening balance sheet as seen in Table *6.6 on page 110*. The "Adjustments" in the opening balance sheet create a pro-forma balance sheet, which is the starting point for the balance sheet projections of the future. The table *Adjustments of Individual Positions* explains the adjustments.

6.6 Balance Sheet (in Mio. USD)

	Opening 2015	Adjustments +	Adjustments -	Pro Forma 2015
Property, Plant and Equipment	800.0			800.0
Goodwill and Intangible Assets	200.0	90.5		290.5
Other Asset	80.0			80.0
Total Fixed Assets	**1,080.0**			**1,170.5**
Cash and Cash Equivalents	50.0		(50.0)	-
Accounts Receivable	180.0			180.0
Inventories	145.0			145.0
Prepaids and Other Current Assets	50.0			50.0
Total Assets	**1,505.0**			**1,545.5**
Ordinary Equity	900.0	10.0	(900.0)	10.0
Fixed Return Instrument	-	480.5		480.5
Retained Earnings	-			-
Total Shareholders Equity	**900.0**			**490.5**
Existing Term Loan	500.0		(500.0)	-
Term Loan C	-	300.0		300.0
Term Loan B	-	300.0		300.0
Term Loan A	-	350.0		350.0
Revolving Credit Facility	-			-
Other Long Term-Liabilities	-			-
Total Long Term Liabilities	**500.0**			**950.0**
Accounts Payable	75.0			75.0
Other Current Liabilities	30.0			30.0
Total Current Liabilities	**105.0**			**105.0**
Total Liabilities and Equity	**1,505.0**			**1,545.5**
Balance Check	**0.0**			**0.0**

Adjustments of Individual Positons		
Position	Info	Calculation
Goodwill and Intangible Assets	Because the purchase price for the equity is higher than the fair value of the equity (here the fair value = book value as a simplification) the difference creates a goodwill which is booked in the balance sheet (further explainations see *Digression: Goodwill*).	990.5 (Purchases TargetCo. Equity) - 900 (Ordinary Equity) = 90.5
Cash and Cash Equivalents	The Cash on Hand which is on the balance sheet is used to pay the purchase price.	
Ordinary Equity	The old equity is taken out of the balance sheet and replayed by the new equity.	
Fixed Return Instrument (FRI)	This is a new position, the FRI is added to the equity in the balance sheet. The FRI in the balance sheet is less than what is written in the *6.5 Sources and Uses of Funds* table. This is because the FRI is paying first of all the Financing Fees and Other Fees and Expenses.	605.5 (FRI) - 95.0 (Financing Fees) - 30.0 (Other Fees and Expenses) = 480.5
Existing Term Loan	Old loans are entirely repayd and taken out of the balance sheet.	
Term Loan A-C	Added to the balance sheet	
Revolving Credit Facility	Added to the balance sheet	

Digression: Goodwill

Generally, a so-called goodwill is created in an acquisition. The goodwill is created when the purchase price is higher as the fair value of the company. In this model, as a simplified assumption, it will be assumed that the goodwill is the difference between the equity purchase price and the equity book value of the company. The book value is regularly lower than the fair value, which means that the goodwill is higher in this model. In a real transaction however, the goodwill will be distributed to the assets (e.g. buildings and machineries) by calculating the fair value of the individual assets. When the goodwill is distributed to the assets and thereby the value of the assets is increased the yearly depreciations on the assets will decrease the tax expenditures, which is an obvious advantage.

Step 3: Creation of debt schedule and link with balance sheet, income statement, and cash flow statement

Creation of the debt schedule

An important part of the LBO model is the incorporation of the debt schedule after the acquisition. After this, the income statement can be finished by calculating EBIT to net income. Furthermore, can the chance in long term debt as well as the change in equity (through the position net income) be calculated in the balance sheet. The cash flow calculation after the transaction can also be calculated.

Table *6.7 on page 114* shows the debt schedule calculations. The revolver (revolving credit facility) has an agreed credit line of maximal USD 100.0 million and a duration of five years. The revolver does not have to be used and the amount used can vary (in this case maximal USD 100.0 million). However, in case the revolver is not used at all, a commitment fee needs to be paid each year (in this case 0.5% of the credit line). If the revolver is used, interest will be chanced in the amount of the LIBOR[32] at that time + a spread of 2.8% (in this example).

Term Loan A will be repaid yearly as written in the debt schedule; however, at least 10% of the initial amount (USD

---

[32] LIBOR = London Interbank Offered Rate. The LIBOR is a rate that some leading banks charge each other for short-term loans. It is also a very often used benchmark for other loans.

350.0 million) needs to be repaid. Should the available cash flows (free cash flows) be larger than the minimum required repayment, this would also be used for the repayment of Loan A. Apart from this, the following conditions exist for the loans:

- Interest for Loan A will be paid annually; the interest rate depends on the LIBOR at that time + the fixed agreed "spread."
- Loan C and B will only be repaid at the end of the duration (bullet payment); however, the interest will be paid annually.
- The fixed-return instrument is also only repaid at duration. Furthermore, no interest payments will be made during the duration, which means that the instrument increases in value each year in the amount of the interest. The instrument has an amount of USD 605.5 million in the debt schedule, which is exactly USD 125.0 million more than the amount written in the balance sheet. This is due to the mentioned transaction fees of USD 125.0 million, which are paid with the instrument.

If the available cash flows are higher than what is needed to repay Loan A, the difference will be booked in the position Cash and Cash Equivalents. The repayments for Loan A will be linked in the cash flow from financing activities and reduce the available cash flows.

6.7 Debt Schedule (in Mio. USD)

	Pro Forma 2015	Year 1 2016	Year 2 2017	Year 3 2018	Year 4 2019	Year 5 2020
Cash flow from Operating Activities		66.0	79.5	94.4	110.9	129.1
Cash flow from Investing Activities (2% of Sales)		(17.9)	(19.0)	(20.1)	(21.2)	(22.5)
Cash Available for mandatory debt repaym.		**48.1**	**60.5**	**74.4**	**89.7**	**106.7**
Mandatory debt repayments		35.0	35.0	35.0	35.0	35.0
Cash available for optional debt repaiments		**13.1**	**25.5**	**39.4**	**54.7**	**71.7**
Cash to Balance Sheet (after repaiments)		0.0	0.0	0.0	0.0	29.3
Forward LIBOR Curve		3.0%	3.15%	3.30%	3.45%	3.60%

Revolving Credit Facility

Size	100.0	Repayment Schedule:	per Annum, at least 10% of beginning Amount			
Spread	2.8%					
Term	5 years					
Commitment Fee on Unused Portio	0.5%					
Beginning Balance		0.0	0.0	0.0	0.0	0.0
Drawdown / (Repayment)		0.0	0.0	0.0	0.0	0.0
Closing Balance		**0.0**	**0.0**	**0.0**	**0.0**	**0.0**
Interest Rate		5.8%	6.0%	6.1%	6.3%	6.4%
Interest Expenses		0.0	0.0	0.0	0.0	0.0
Commitment Fee		0.5	0.5	0.5	0.5	0.5

Term Loan A

Amount	350.0	Repayment Schedule:	per Annum, at least 10% of beginning Amount			
Spread	3.0%					
Term	5 years					
Beginning Balance		350.0	301.9	241.4	167.1	77.4
Repayment		48.1	60.5	74.4	89.7	77.4
Closing Balance		**301.9**	**241.4**	**167.1**	**77.4**	**0.0**
Interest Rate (LIBOR + Spread)		6.0%	6.2%	6.3%	6.5%	6.6%
Interest Expenses		21.0	18.6	15.2	10.8	5.1

Term Loan B

Amount	300.0	Repayment Schedule:	Bullet at Maturity			
Spread	3.5%					
Term	7 years					
Beginning Balance		300.0	300.0	300.0	300.0	300.0
Repayment		0.0	0.0	0.0	0.0	0.0
Closing Balance		**300.0**	**300.0**	**300.0**	**300.0**	**300.0**
Interest Rate (LIBOR + Spread)		6.5%	6.7%	6.8%	7.0%	7.1%
Interest Expenses		19.5	20.0	20.4	20.9	21.3

Term Loan C

Amount	300.0	Repayment Schedule: Bullet at Maturity					
Spread	4.0%						
Term	8 years						
Beginning Balance			300.0	300.0	300.0	300.0	300.0
Repayment			0.0	0.0	0.0	0.0	0.0
Closing Balance			300.0	300.0	300.0	300.0	300.0
Interest Rate (LIBOR + Spread)			7.0%	7.2%	7.3%	7.5%	7.6%
Interest Expenses			21.0	21.5	21.9	22.4	22.8

Fix Return Instrument (Sharholder Loan)

Amount	605.5	Repayment Schedule: Accumulating, Bullet at Maturity					
Pricing	12.5%						
Term	8 years						
Beginning Balance			605.5	681.2	766.3	862.1	969.9
Repayment			0.0	0.0	0.0	0.0	0.0
Interest Expenses			75.7	85.1	95.8	107.8	121.2
Closing Balance			681.2	766.3	862.1	969.9	1,091.1

Completion of the income statement from EBIT to net income

In order to complete the income statement calculation, the interest expenses from the debt schedule need to be linked in the income statement. **Cash Interest Expenses** are interest expenses that actually lead to a cash flow and are the interest expenses of Term Loans A to C and the revolver. Furthermore, the non-cash interest of the Fixed Return Instrument (FRI) is considered. This needs to be accounting-wise correct as the interest needs to be considered in the income statement in the year in which it occurs. As already mentioned, this is positively considered in the cash flow calculation. Table *6.8 on page 117* shows the complete income statement. As can be seen in the table, in 2016 the cash interest expenses amounted to USD 62.0 million. Altogether USD 137.7 million in net interest expenses were paid (interest income is subtracted from the interest expenses, resulting in the net interest expenses. In this model, however, there is no interest income).

For the calculation of the tax expenses it is assumed that the interest expenses for the FRI are not tax-deductible. This is the case if the instrument is seen as equity. The taxable income is calculated by adding the EBT (earnings before taxes) with the fixed-return instrument interest. 30% are used as the tax rate. In 2016 the tax expenditures amount to USD 25.1 million.

The net income in all years from 2015 to 2020 are all negative. This is among others due to the interest expenses for the FRI. The negative net income will be linked in the balance sheet in the position Retained Earnings and reduce the equity. However, since the non-cash interests of the FRI are higher than the negative net income, is the equity increasing every year (as can be seen in the balance sheet in Table 6.9 *on page 118*).

6.8 Income Statement (in Mio. USD)

	Pro Forma 2015	Year 1 2016	Year 2 2017	Year 3 2018	Year 4 2019	Year 5 2020
Revenue	845.0	894.9	947.7	1,003.6	1,061.8	1,123.4
% growth	*5.9%*	*5.9%*	*5.9%*	*5.9%*	*5.8%*	*5.8%*
Cost of Goods Sold	431.0	456.4	483.3	511.8	541.5	572.9
Gross profit	414.1	438.5	464.3	491.7	520.3	550.4
Gross profit margin (%)	*49.0%*	*49.0%*	*49.0%*	*49.0%*	*49.0%*	*49.0%*
Operating expenses	281.0	289.4	298.1	307.1	316.3	325.8
Other income	14.5	14.5	14.5	14.5	14.5	14.5
EBITDA	147.6	163.5	180.7	199.2	218.5	239.2
EBITDA margin (%)	*17.5%*	*18.3%*	*19.1%*	*19.8%*	*20.6%*	*21.3%*
Depreciation & Amortisation	16.9	17.9	19.0	20.1	21.2	22.5
EBIT	130.7	145.7	161.8	179.1	197.3	216.7
Interest Expenses						
Revolving Credit Facility (Revolver)	0.0	0.0	0.0	0.0	0.0	0.0
Commitment Fees on Unused Rev.	0.5	0.5	0.5	0.5	0.5	0.5
Term Loan A	21.0	21.0	18.6	15.2	10.8	5.1
Term Loan B	19.5	19.5	20.0	20.4	20.9	21.3
Term Loan C	21.0	21.0	21.5	21.9	22.4	22.8
Total Cash Interest Expense	62.0	62.0	60.5	58.0	54.5	49.7
Fix Return Instrument (FRI) Interest	75.7	75.7	85.1	95.8	107.8	121.2
Interest Income	0.0	0.0	0.0	0.0	0.0	0.0
Net Interest Expense	137.7	137.7	145.6	153.8	162.2	170.9
Earnings Before Taxes (EBT)		8.0	16.2	25.3	35.0	45.8
Taxible income (EBT+non-deductible FRI interest)		83.7	101.3	121.1	142.8	167.0
Tax Expense (30% of Taxible income)		25.1	30.4	36.3	42.8	50.1
Net Income		-17.1	-14.2	-11.0	-7.8	-4.3

Completion of the balance sheet

The balance sheet is completed by linking the closing balance of the individual debt instruments as well as the FRI from the debt schedule in the balance sheet. Since only Loan A is repaid, it is the only loan that decreases in the balance sheet. FRI increases due to the accumulation of the interest. Table *6.9 on page 118* shows the complete balance sheet. As mentioned and shown in the table, the net income from the income statement is subsumed under Retained Earnings. In 2016, this resulted in negative Retained Earnings of USD 17.1 million (which is the negative net income of 2016). The negative Retained Earnings thereby increase each year by the negative net income of that year.

Goodwill and Intangible Assets are held constant here as a simplifying assumption. In reality, chances would likely occur through the yearly impairment test.

6.9 Balance Sheet (in Mio. USD)					
	Year 1 2016	Year 2 2017	Year 3 2018	Year 4 2019	Year 5 2020
Property, Plant and Equipment	800.0	800.0	800.0	800.0	800.0
Goodwill and Intangible Assets	290.5	290.5	290.5	290.5	290.5
Other Asset	80.0	80.0	80.0	80.0	80.0
Total Fixed Assets	**1,170.5**	**1,170.5**	**1,170.5**	**1,170.5**	**1,170.5**
Cash and Cash Equivalents	0.0	0.0	0.0	0.0	29.3
Accounts Receivable	188.0	196.0	203.9	211.8	219.6
Inventories	156.0	166.9	177.7	188.3	198.9
Prepaids and Other Current Assets	50.5	50.8	51.1	51.3	51.5
Total Assets	**1,565.0**	**1,584.2**	**1,603.1**	**1,621.9**	**1,669.8**
Ordinary Equity	10.0	10.0	10.0	10.0	10.0
Fixed Return Instrument	556.2	641.3	737.1	844.9	966.1
Retained Earnings	-17.1	-31.4	-42.4	-50.2	-54.5
Total Shareholders Equity	**549.1**	**620.0**	**704.8**	**804.7**	**921.6**
Existing Term Loan	0.0	0.0	0.0	0.0	0.0
Term Loan C	300.0	300.0	300.0	300.0	300.0
Term Loan B	300.0	300.0	300.0	300.0	300.0
Term Loan A	301.9	241.4	167.1	77.4	0.0
Revolving Credit Facility	0.0	0.0	0.0	0.0	0.0
Other Long Term Liabilities	0.0	0.0	0.0	0.0	0.0
Total Long Term Liabilities	**901.9**	**841.4**	**767.1**	**677.4**	**600.0**
Accounts Payable	82.0	88.9	95.8	102.7	109.5
Other Current Liabilities	32.0	33.8	35.5	37.1	38.6
Total Current Liabilities	**114.0**	**122.7**	**131.3**	**139.8**	**148.2**
Total Liabilities and Equity	**1,565.0**	**1,584.2**	**1,603.1**	**1,621.9**	**1,669.8**
Balance Check	0.0	0.0	0.0	0.0	0.0

Completion of the cash flow calculation

In order to complete the cash flow calculation, the cash flow from financing activities needs to be completed. The repayment of Loan A is considered here, which is linked from the debt schedule to the cash flow calculation. The *Ending Cash Balance* is linked, as already mentioned, to the balance sheet to position *Cash and Cash Equivalents*. Table *6.10 on page 120* shows the cash flow calculation. As can be seen, in year 2020, the available cash amounts to USD 29.3 million. This amount also increases the Cash and Cash Equivalents position in the balance sheet to USD 29.3 million.

6.10 Cash flow Statement (in Mio. USD)

	Year 1 2016	Year 2 2017	Year 3 2018	Year 4 2019	Year 5 2020
Operating Activities					
Net income	(17.1)	(14.2)	(11.0)	(7.8)	(4.3)
Plus: Depreciation & Amortization	17.9	19.0	20.1	21.2	22.5
Plus: Non Cash Interest of FRI	75.7	85.1	95.8	107.8	121.2
Change in Working Capital items					
(Inc.) / Dec. in Accounts Receivable	(8.0)	(8.0)	(7.9)	(7.9)	(7.8)
(Inc.) / Dec. in Inventories	(11.0)	(10.9)	(10.8)	(10.7)	(10.6)
(Inc.) / Dec. in Other Current Assets	(0.5)	(0.3)	(0.3)	(0.2)	(0.2)
Inc. / (Dec.) in Accounts Payable	7.0	6.9	6.9	6.9	6.8
Inc. / (Dec.) in Other Current Liabilities	2.0	1.8	1.7	1.6	1.5
(Inc.) / Dec. in Net Working Capital	(10.5)	(10.4)	(10.4)	(10.3)	(10.2)
Cash flow from Operating Activities	**66.0**	**79.5**	**94.4**	**110.9**	**129.1**
Investing Activities					
Capital Expenditures	(17.9)	(19.0)	(20.1)	(21.2)	(22.5)
Other Investing Activities	0.0	0.0	0.0	0.0	0.0
Cash flow from Investing Activities	**(17.9)**	**(19.0)**	**(20.1)**	**(21.2)**	**(22.5)**
Financing Activities					
Equity Issuance / (Repurchase)	0.0	0.0	0.0	0.0	0.0
Dividends	0.0	0.0	0.0	0.0	0.0
Existing Term Loan	0.0	0.0	0.0	0.0	0.0
Term Loan C	0.0	0.0	0.0	0.0	0.0
Term Loan B	0.0	0.0	0.0	0.0	0.0
Term Loan A	(48.1)	(60.5)	(74.4)	(89.7)	(77.4)
Revolving Credit Facility	0.0	0.0	0.0	0.0	0.0
Cash flow from Financing Activites	**(48.1)**	**(60.5)**	**(74.4)**	**(89.7)**	**(77.4)**
Excess Cash for the Period	0.0	0.0	0.0	0.0	29.3
Beginning Cash Balance	0.0	0.0	0.0	0.0	0.0
Ending Cash Balance	**0.0**	**0.0**	**0.0**	**0.0**	**29.3**

Step 4: Performing LBO analysis and return calculation

Before the return calculation (so answering the question what the private equity fund and its investors will earn on the transaction) can be done, it needs to be investigated if the main covenants were fulfilled.

The exact characteristics of the covenants are agreed with the debt providers. If the covenants are not fulfilled, more equity needs to be provided, or it could be tried to get cheaper debt instruments (with maybe better repayment characteristics).

Table *6.1* at the beginning of this chapter shows the often-used covenants under the point *Summary Credit Stats*. Since the EBITDA increases and Loan A is reduced each year, the covenants improve each year too. The covenant of *free cash flow of the last 12 months (LTM) / debt service* (cash interest and debt repayments) is generally agreed on at least one time. In 2016 this covenant is 1.1 times above the minimum requirement and therefore fulfilled.

This means that, in this scenario, the company is able to serve the level of debt, whereby the financial structure can be accepted.

However, in the investigation of covenants, different scenarios should be calculated. In particular, it should be checked if the profitability of the company decreases (due to internal or external factors), the covenants can still be fulfilled.

Owing to the modelling, and because all relevant positions are linked together, it is easy to calculate different scenarios in Excel (LBO analysis). For example, if the level of debt and equity is changed, the cost of debt will increase or decrease, or the debt repayment schedule could be changed. Another possible analysis is to see what happens when the sale price per unit is reduced (decrease of revenue), but the costs remain the same, which would lead to a reduced EBITDA margin.

Return analysis

At the end of the LBO valuation, it is calculated what returns the private equity fund, the investors, and the company's management are likely to make with the transaction. In this model, it is assumed that the exit multiple is the same as the entry multiple (so valuations basically stay the same). In a sensitivity analysis, however, it is often calculated with slightly lower or higher multiples.

The following exit waterfall shows how the proceeds are distributed after an exit. The EV (enterprise value) results from the multiplication of the multiple with EBITDA of the exit year. In 2020 the EBITDA is USD 239.2 million. Multiplied by 10.0 (exit multiple), it results in an enterprise value of USD 2,391.9 million (not 2,392 based on precise Excel calculations).

Exit waterfall (in million USD)

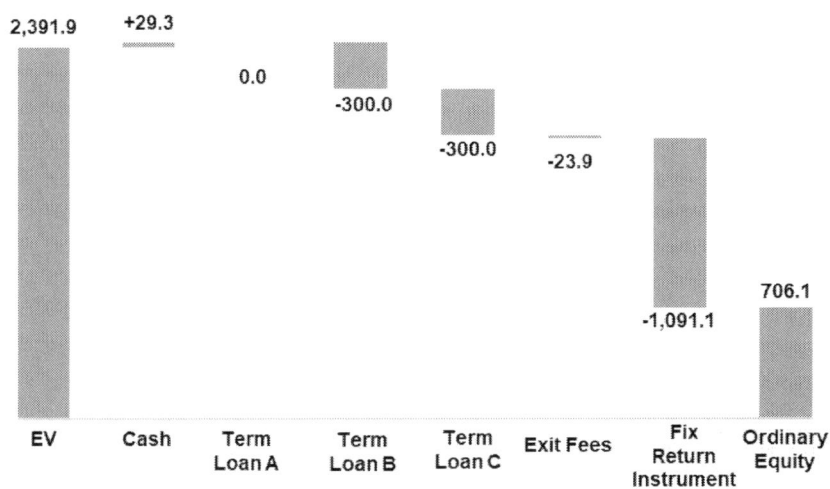

As can be seen from the waterfall, the loans are paid first (Loan A is 0 as it is repaid already). The exit fees are fees which occur because of the exit (e.g. consulting fees for investment banker and lawyer). Here it is assumed that the fees make 1% of the enterprise value.

The FRI is paid back to the private equity fund (respectively the funds investors). Out of the remaining ordinary equity of USD 706.1 million, 80% is paid to the private equity fund and 20% to the management (sweet equity). Therefore, the private equity fund receives USD 564.9 million (USD 706.1 million * 80%) and the management USD 141.2 million.

As can be seen, the profit for the management is huge. It invested USD 2 million and received, after five years USD 141.2 million back. This (realistic) example shows that a private equity transaction can be very rewarding for the management. However, this is only the case if the management is managing the company well and increases its value significantly.

Indicators to measure returns

Besides other indicators for the return measurement, the money multiple and the internal rate of return (IRR) are very often used indicators. These will be explained in the following.

Money multiple

This indicator shows to what extent the private equity fund was able to multiply the invested capital and it is calculated in the following manner:

$$\frac{\text{Capital after exit}}{\text{Capital invested in the company}} = \frac{\text{USD } 1{,}656.0 \text{ m}}{\text{USD } 613.5 \text{ m}} = 2.7\text{x}$$

The capital after exit is calculated by adding the FRI (USD 1,091.1 million) to the 80% of the ordinary equity (USD 564.9 million).

With this transaction, the invested capital could therefore be multiplied by a factor of 2.7. For comparison, the private equity firm Permira earned a money multiple of 2.3 times with the Hugo Boss AG investment (sold in 2015) and a money multiple of 4.2 times with Premiere AG (a private TV channel from Germany which was renamed Sky) investment (sold in 2006).

<u>Internal Rate of Return (IRR)</u>

The IRR calculates the average yearly return and is calculated by finding the interest rate (i), which sets the net present value to 0. The formula is as follows:

$$\text{Net present value} = -invested\ capital + \sum_{t=1}^{T} \frac{Cash\ flow_t}{(1+i)^t} = 0$$

T = time frame where the cash flows occur (here five years); i = wanted interest rate (IRR)

A formula for doing this calculation is done in Excel. For the calculated investment, the IRR after five years is 22% (*see Table 6.11 on page 125*). Many private equity funds say that they target an IRR of around 25%, so the investment's IRR is only slightly below the favored return. However, this is also due to the fact that no dividend payments or alike are considered in this model. Often a portfolio company distributes money during the holding period to the private equity fund (e.g. through dividend recapitalization; see next pages for more information about dividend recapitalization), which would increase the IRR since positive payouts would be done earlier.

It should be noted that the IRR is absolutely time-sensitive. Keeping everything else equal but selling the company after four years, the IRR increases to 28.2%. If the company is sold only after six years, the IRR decreases to 18.0%.

Table *6.11* shows the IRR calculation for a five-year holding period:

6.11 IRR Calculation (in Mio. USD)						
	2015	2016	2017	2018	2019	2020
Equity investment	(613.5)					
Dividend / (additional Equity)	0.0	0.0	0.0	0.0	0.0	0.0
Equity value at Exit						1,656.0
Sum	(613.5)	0.0	0.0	0.0	0.0	1,656.0
IRR	22.0%					

Profit for the investor and the general partner of the fund

Table *6.12 on page 126* shows what calculations are needed to get the amount of profit the investor and the general partner of the fund is making. The fund's investors, who provided USD 613.5 million in equity capital (FRI and ordinary equity), will get after the management fee and the carry for the general partner USD 1,321.0 million after five years. The general partner, who did not invest any money in the fund (simplified assumption; in reality, the general partner always invests money in the fund), will receive through the management fee and the carry a return of USD 335.0 million[33,34].

6.12 Profit for Investor and the General Partner of the Fund (in Mio. USD)

	2015	2016	2017	2018	2019	2020
Equity investment	(613.5)					
Equity at Exit						1,656.0
2.0% p.a. Management Fee		12.3	12.3	12.3	12.3	12.3
Sum of Management Fee						61.4
8.0% p.a. Hurdle Rate		49.1	53.0	57.2	61.8	66.8
Sum of Hurdle Rate						287.9
Profit after Hurdle Rate						1,368.1
80.0% of Profit for Investor						1,094.5
20.0% Carry for Private Equity Fund						273.6
Sum of Profits for Investor (after Management Fee)						1,321.0
Sum of Profits for Private Equity Fund						335.0

Dividend recapitalization

Many private equity funds go for a dividend recapitalization after they have remained invested in a company for a few years. In a dividend recapitalization, a significant amount is paid to the

---

[33] For an explanation of the management fee, hurdle rate, and carry, see Chapter 1

[34] In this example, the hurdle rate is not actually paid out during 2016–2019 but only in 2020. The sum of the hurdle rate payments is thus a bit higher due to the compounded interest until 2020 on the 8.0% in 2016, 2017, 2018, and 2019. Often a company would pay out some dividends during the holding period, which the fund would directly distribute to the investors as a hurdle rate payment.

fund as a special dividend. This dividend is financed by the company with new debt which it issues. Since after a few years the company has paid back some of the acquisition debt, it is possible to take out new debt. Furthermore, the company is likely to grow over the years, which allows it to secure additional debt. If the debt amounts to USD 100.0 million right after the acquisition, and if USD 30.0 million are repaid after three years, the company can take out another USD 100 million in debt. Out of that USD 100 million, USD 70 million will repay the old loan and USD 30 million will be paid as a special dividend to the private equity fund. Fees could be charged due to the early repayment of the old debt. What is more, the debt level will increase to the approximately same level as it was after the acquisition. This, again, will put pressure on the management to be not wasteful with the cash flows. They will only invest in projects that will most likely increase the value of the company.

For the private equity fund, dividend recapitalization has the obvious advantages as it already gets some of the investment money back (reduced risk). What is more, it increases the IRR as a positive cash flow occurs already after three years.

References

Achleitner, A. K., Braun, R., Engel, N., Figge, C., & Tappeiner, F.: Value creation drivers in private equity buyouts: Empirical evidence from Europe. The Journal of Private Equity, **2010**

Auerbach, J., ed. Mergers and acquisitions. University of Chicago Press, 2008

Balz, U.; Arlinghaus, O: Praxisbuch Mergers & Acquisitions. Von der strategischen Überlegung zur erfolgreichen Integration, 2. Aufl., Landsberg am Lech: mi-Fachverlag, **2007**

Bayaz, D: Heuschrecken zwischen Rendite, Reportage und Regulierung. Die Bedeutung von Private Equity in Ökonomie und Öffentlichkeit, Springer Fachmedien Wiesbaden, **2014**

Becker, A. Private Equity Buyout Funds-Value Creation in Portfoliounternehmen. vol.Vol. 391. Haupt Verlag AG, **2009**

Brettel, M.; Hiddemann, T.; Meier, D.: Wertsteigerung bei Buyouts in der Post Investment-Phase – der Beitrag von Private Equity Firmen zum operativen Erfolg ihrer Portfoliounternehmen im Europäischen Vergleich, ZfB Zeitschrift für Betriebswirtschaft, Gabor-Verlag, **2006**

Brettel, M.; Kauffmann, C.; Kühn, C.; Sobczak, C: Private Equity-Investoren. Eine Einführung, 1.Aufl., Stuttgart: W. Kohlhammer, **2008**

Caselli, S. Private equity and venture capital in Europe: markets, techniques, and deals. Academic Press, **2009**

Damodaran, A. Applied corporate finance. John Wiley & Sons, **2010**

Diller, C. Private Equity: Rendite, Risiko und Markteinflussfaktoren: eine empirische Analyse Europäischer Private-Equity-Fonds. Uhlenbruch, **2007**

Eilers, S.; Koffka, M.; Mackensen, M: Private Equity. Unternehmenskauf – Finanzierung – Restrukturierung - Exitstrategien, München: Verlag C.H. Beck, **2009**

Ernst, D., and Häcker, J. Applied international corporate finance.

Vahlen, **2012**

Finkel, R. and David G. The masters of private equity Private Equity and venture capital. McGraw Hill Professional, **2009**

Geidner, A. Der Wandel der Unternehmensführung in Buyouts: Eine Untersuchung Private-Equity-finanzierter Desinvestitionen. Springer-Verlag, **2009**

Göppert, A. and Müller, C. "Finanzierung mittelständischer Unternehmen durch Private Equity." Finanzierungsstrategien im Mittelstand. Springer Fachmedien Wiesbaden, **2014**

Gündel, M., and Katzorke, B. Private Equity: Finanzierungsinstrument und Anlagemöglichkeit. Bank-Verlag Medien GmbH, **2007**

Just, L.: Private Equity. Die Auswirkungen von Private Equity auf Wachstum und Beschäftigung, Saarrücken: VDM Verlag Dr. Müller, **2006**

Klamer, N.; Sommer, U.; Weber, I.: Der effiziente M&A Prozess. Die Acquisition Value Chain, 1. Aufl., Freiburg: Haufe, 2013

Landau, C: Wertschöpfungsbeiträge durch Private-Equity-Gesellschaften. Empirische Untersuchung Europäischer Spin-off-Buyouts, 1. Aufl., Springer Fachmedien Wiesbaden, **2010**

Pearl, J. and Rosenbaum J. Investment banking: valuation, leveraged buyouts, and mergers and acquisitions. John Wiley & Sons, **2013**

Pignataro, P. Leveraged Buyouts: A Practical Guide to Investment Banking and Private Equity. John Wiley & Sons, **2014**

Pignataro, P. Financial modeling and valuation: A practical guide to investment banking and private equity. John Wiley & Sons, **2013**

Sari, E: Die steuerliche Behandlung der Verschmelzung von einer Kapitalgesellschaft auf eine andere Kapitalgesellschaft, Hamburg: Diplomica Verlag GmbH, **2013**

Schlitt, M., ed. Finanzierungsstrategien im Mittelstand. Springer-Verlag, **2014**

Schneck, O: Handbuch Alternativer Finanzierungsformen, 1. Aufl., Weinheim: Wiley-Vech, **2006**

Seckler, D.; Seitz C.: Leitfaden M&A und Fusionskontrolle: Praktische Rechtstipps für Unternehmenskauf und –verkauf, Linde Verlag Wien, **2011**

Siebert, J.; Lickert, D.: Diskussionsbeitrag. Handels- und steuerrechtliche Behandlung eines Forderungsverzichts mit Besserungsschein und eines Rangrücktritts bei der GmbH. Herausgeber: Prof. Dr. Wolfgang Hirschberger, **2006**

Stadler, W.: Venture Capital und Private Equity. Erfolgreich wachsen mit Beteiligungskapital, Köln: Fachverlag Deutscher Wirtschaftsdienst, **2000**

Steinbrenner, H: Professionelle Optionsgeschäfte. Moderne Bewertungsmethoden richtig verstehen, Wien/Frankfurt: Wirtschaftsverlag Ueberreuter, **2001**

Thum, O., Timmreck, C. and Keul, T. "Private Equity."Leitfaden zur erfolgreichen Unternehmensfinanzierung. München: Vahlen, **2008**

Weber, T.; Hohaus, B: Buy-outs. Funktionsweise, Strukturierung, Bewertung und Umsetzung von Unternehmenstransaktionen, 1. Aufl., Stuttgart: Schäffer-Poeschel Verlag, **2010**

Werner, H: Mezzanine-Kapital. Mit Mezzanine-Finanzierung die Eigenkapitalquote erhöhen, 2. Aufl., Köln: Bank-Verlag, **2007**

Literature recommendation for LBO valuations

Ernst, D., and Häcker, J. *Applied international corporate finance.* Vahlen, 2012.

- The book describes the M&A procedure very comprehensively. What is more, it explains LBO valuation. The book is written in English; however, it translates important terms into German.

Pearl, J. and Rosenbaum J. *Investment banking: valuation, leveraged buyouts, and mergers and acquisitions.* John Wiley & Sons, 2013.

- The book describes the LBO process very comprehensively and provides an LBO model case study. It uses US GAAP as accounting standard.

Pignataro, P. *Leveraged buyouts: A practical guide to investment banking and private equity.* John Wiley & Sons, 2014.

- The book does what it promises in the title. This book is very practical and shows LBO valuation in a practical way too. An excellent model can be downloaded from the book's website.

Pignataro, P. *Financial modeling and valuation: A practical guide to investment banking and private equity.* John Wiley & Sons, 2013.

- A very good book about modeling that also shows other valuation methods than LBO valuation. Furthermore, it answers general questions about accounting.

Glossary

Add-on acquisition: A private equity fund might use add-on acquisitions to increase the value of a portfolio company. In that case, the portfolio company will acquire another company which will lead to a value increase for the combined company. The add-on target is selected with the help of the private equity fund. The fund will also support during the acquisition negotiations. Sometimes the fund even provides some capital to meet the add-on target.

Capital call: When the private equity fund wants to make an investment, it demands its investors to provide the money, which is called a capital call. When the fund is created investors only pledge the money and only pay it when it is needed.

Co-investment: Sometimes some investors of the private equity fund (limited partners, e.g. pension funds) invest capital directly in a target company (along with the fund). This is called a co-investment. The investors thereby carry more risk since they are invested with a larger amount in one company. However, they are also participating more when the target company increases in value. Furthermore, they do not have to pay any management fee to the private equity fund for the invested amount. For the private equity fund, a co-investment can be attractive when they want to acquire a large company which they could not acquire with only the fund's capital.

Commitment: The maximum amount an investor will be required to invest in the fund. On average, funds draw approximately 90% of the committed amount within the first four to six years of a fund's life. Distributions (from dividends or sales proceeds) are expected before the full amount of the commitment is called.

Distribution: Capital distributed to a fund's investors as underlying investments is realized. Usually, an investor will receive his/her initial investment plus a preferred return before the general partner can participate in the profits. Such arrangements are specified in the Limited Partnership Agreement and are referred to as "distribution waterfall."
(more details on p. 23 and 123)

Free-riding principle: In the private equity context, it means that the private equity fund manager is increasing the value of the portfolio company from which also other shareholder profit from. However, these shareholders do not work for it. When the general partner is paid a monitoring fee, the free-riding principle becomes void, as the other shareholders indirectly (via the portfolio company) pay the general partner for its work.
(more details on p. 29 and 90)

Hedge funds: Hedge funds pool investors' money (as private equity funds do) and invest it, unlike private equity funds, mainly on the stock market. There are many hedge funds with many different strategies to invest the money (e.g. short-sale hedge funds). Often investors can demand the provided capital back

within a view month.
(more details on p. 12)

Internal rate of return (IRR): The annual compounded rate of return of the investments in the fund. Net IRR is earned by investors net of fees and carry.

Invested capital: The amount of the commitment that has actually been invested in the portfolio company.

Leverage effect: The leverage effect is the effect that the debt has on the equity return. When the cost of debt (e.g. 5%) is lower than the return on investment (e.g. 15% because the company receives a 15% return on the debt and equity invested), an increase in the amount of debt can increase the equity return. However, the leverage effect also works in the negative direction. When the return on investment is lower than the cost of debt, the equity return will decrease. Depending on how much debt the company is using, it could result in serious financial distress. The leverage effect is routinely used by private equity funds.

Monitoring fee: A fee private equity funds often charge to portfolio companies for the advice they provide.
(more details on p. 90)

NAV (Net asset value): The value of investments based on the private equity fund's valuation guidelines. This value is rarely correlated to the commitment amount. The NAV in itself is not an indicator of fund performance as it does not reflect the levels of capital calls and disbursements.

Residual value paid-in (RVPI) multiple: The valuation of unrealized investments (i.e. portfolio companies that are not sold yet) as a percentage of called capital.

Short sale: Most investors acquire stocks to bet on an increase in a stock price. However, if an investor believes a stock will decrease in value, he can do a short sale. In a short sale, the investor will borrow stocks from another investor (often from banks), which he then sells on the stock exchange. After a certain time, the investor needs to return the stocks to the borrower. He buys the stocks on the stock exchange and returns them to the borrower. The investor hopes to sell the stocks at a higher price as he has to buy them later (he hopes for a fall in the stock price).

Sweet equity: In order to have an alignment of interests, the portfolio company management acquires a share in the company. However, the management most often does not have enough money to acquire a meaningful share in the company. Sweet equity thus allows them to acquire equity for a discount (compared to what the private equity fund will pay for the equity). (more details on p. 66 and 123)

Vintage: The first year in which a commitment is made. As the fund invests over several years, this simply indicates the starting point of the investment period.

About the author

Daniel Burmester is a best-selling author in Germany. In 2016, he published the first version of the private equity book. He is currently working as a consultant in a global strategy consulting firm where he consults large banks and other financial institutions. He has worked and studied in five different countries. His work stations have included an international private equity fund of funds, the mergers & acquisitions departments of investment banks, and a role in one of the "Big Four" accounting firms. He has consulted private equity funds of different sizes and in different geographies. Furthermore, he has published articles in an international magazine about company valuations. Daniel holds a double master's degree in international finance and financial economics.

Made in the USA
Lexington, KY
30 April 2019